# A Simple Guide to SPSS/PC+®

*For Versions 4.0 and 5.0*

*Lee A. Kirkpatrick* is assistant professor of psychology at The College of William & Mary in Williamsburg, Virginia. He received his B.S. from Lynchburg College, his M.A. in general/experimental psychology from the University of Texas at El Paso, and his Ph.D. in social/personality psychology from the University of Denver. His research interests include adult attachment, close relationships, the psychology of religion, and evolutionary psychology. Dr. Kirkpatrick teaches undergraduate and graduate courses in statistics and research methods.

*Brooke C. Feeney* is pursuing her Ph.D. in social psychology at the State University of New York at Buffalo, after receiving her B.A. from Salisbury State University and her M.A. in general/experimental psychology from The College of William & Mary. As a graduate teaching assistant at William & Mary, she developed, for use by undergraduate students in elementary statistics courses, an extensive set of handouts on SPSS/PC+, from which this manual eventually evolved.

# *A Simple Guide to SPSS/PC+®*

*For Versions 4.0 and 5.0*

*Lee A. Kirkpatrick*
The College of William & Mary

*Brooke C. Feeney*
State University of New York at Buffalo

Brooks/Cole Publishing Company
I(T)P™ An International Thomson Publishing Company

Pacific Grove • Albany • Bonn • Boston • Cincinnati • Detroit • London • Madrid • Melbourne
Mexico City • New York • Paris • San Francisco • Singapore • Tokyo • Toronto • Washington

Sponsoring Editor: *Jim Brace-Thompson*
Marketing Team: *Margaret Parks and Gay Meixel*
Marketing Representative: *Bob Podstepny*
Production Coordinator: *Fiorella Ljunggren*
Production: *Scratchgravel Publishing Services*
Manuscript Editor: *Carol Reitz*
Permissions Editor: *Carline Haga*
Interior Design: *Anne Draus, Scratchgravel Publishing Services*
Cover Design: *Roy R. Neuhaus*
Typesetting: *Scratchgravel Publishing Services*
Printing and Binding: *Malloy Lithographing, Inc.*



*For more information, contact:*

BROOKS/COLE PUBLISHING COMPANY
511 Forest Lodge Road
Pacific Grove, CA 93950
USA

International Thomson Publishing Europe
Berkshire House 168-173
High Holborn
London WC1V 7AA
England

Thomas Nelson Australia
102 Dodds Street
South Melbourne, 3205
Victoria, Australia

Nelson Canada
1120 Birchmount Road
Scarborough, Ontario
Canada M1K 5G4

International Thomson Editores
Campos Eliseos 385, Piso 7
Col. Polanco
11560 México D. F. México

International Thomson Publishing GmbH
Königswinterer Strasse 418
53227 Bonn
Germany

International Thomson Publishing Asia
221 Henderson Road
#05-10 Henderson Building
Singapore 0315

International Thomson Publishing Japan
Hirakawacho Kyowa Building, 3F
2-2-1 Hirakawacho
Chiyoda-ku, Tokyo 102
Japan



Printed in the United States of America

10 9 8 7 6 5 4 3 2

**Library of Congress Cataloging-in-Publication Data**

Kirkpatrick, Lee A., [date]
A simple guide to SPSS/PC+ for versions 4.0 and 5.0 / Lee A. Kirkpatrick, Brooke C. Feeney.
p. cm.
ISBN 0-534-34050-4 (alk. paper)
1. SPSS/PC. (Computer file) 2. Social sciences—Statistical methods—Computer programs. I. Feeney, Brooke C., [date]– . II. Title.
HA32.K57 1996
300'.285'5369—dc20 95-35565
CIP

# Contents

# *Preface*

A tremendous variety of computer software options are available for use in introductory statistics and research methods courses. Although programs designed specifically for teaching purposes and ease of use have obvious advantages, there are also good reasons to prefer a more advanced, research-oriented program such as SPSS/PC+. First, SPSS/PC+ is used very widely, so if one moves to another setting to finish college, pursue a graduate education, or work in applied research, the odds are good that SPSS/PC+ will be available at the new location. Second, learning a powerful program such as SPSS/PC+ in an introductory course prepares the student for data analysis in subsequent advanced courses as well as in "real" research projects later on. It might be a little rough at first, but in the long run the extra investment of time and effort will pay off.

One problem frequently encountered in this context, however, is that of documentation. Large and sophisticated computer programs inevitably require large and sophisticated documentation to explain the many ins and outs of the program. Complete documentation for SPSS/PC+, for instance, includes several weighty and expensive manuals. For students just starting out who wish to use the program for relatively simple tasks such as homework problems or small independent research projects, existing program manuals may be intimidating, confusing, and downright frustrating. If you just want to calculate a quick correlation coefficient or *t*-test for a dozen subjects, you shouldn't have to spend an afternoon perusing three volumes to figure out how to accomplish this. Our goal in writing this manual is to offer an easier alternative to first-time and casual users of SPSS/PC+.

Other books and manuals have been published with similar intentions, but we have not found one that has accomplished the goal as simply and inexpensively as we think should be possible. Some, for example, give equal coverage to other computer programs; the reader interested only in SPSS/PC+ must sift through (and pay for!) the irrelevant pages to find what he or she needs. Other books attempt to achieve a level of comprehensiveness paralleling that of the program itself, delving into advanced multivariate techniques, complicated data transformation procedures, and other topics that are of little value to the beginning student. In addition, most of these books include large amounts of explanatory text between examples of actual computer applications. Although there is surely much to be said for a thorough, conceptual approach to any topic, the fact is that most students (for good reason) just want to know how to get the job done.

This manual was prepared specifically for the beginning student and with an extremely practical orientation in mind. In terms of content, we have tried to include all the major statistical analyses typically covered in an introductory statistics course. In terms of format, our goal was essentially to create an anthology of examples. For each type of analysis, we present (1) a sample problem such as one might find at the end of a textbook chapter, (2) an SPSS/PC+ program designed to read the data and conduct the analysis, and (3) portions of the output produced by the program. Brief explanatory notes are interspersed throughout to clarify and explain details of input and output. We assume that once the example is understood, it should be a relatively simple matter for students to adapt the sample program to their own needs by substituting their own data for the sample data.

We should make clear that we have assiduously avoided discussing the interpretation and meaning of statistical analyses and results. We assume that this material will be covered in a separate textbook and in class lectures and in different ways by different instructors. Some computer manuals delve so deeply into the mathematics and theory behind the statistical procedures that this material may interfere with what is being taught in class. In this manual, we attempt to provide just enough explanation of procedures and outputs to permit students to map this information onto their classroom and textbook knowledge. We also assume that additional support will be provided by the instructor, teaching assistants, or both. This manual is intended merely as a supplemental reference to help instructors, teaching assistants, and students do what they would be doing anyway.

The first section of the manual provides an overview of SPSS/PC+ and some general information about how the program works. There are many different ways in which data and commands can be submitted to SPSS/PC+ and many different ways of viewing and printing program output. Rather than attempt to detail all these alternatives, we describe only what we believe to be the easiest procedure for each. Our intention is not to explore the bewildering array of options but rather to produce the simplest how-to instructions possible. Some more advanced features and procedures are discussed in the appendixes.

Good luck, and happy computing!

## *Acknowledgments*

We would like to thank the following reviewers of the manuscript for their helpful suggestions: Cole Barton of Davidson College, Nicholas Esposito of State University College at Cortland, William Frederickson of the University of Central Oklahoma, Donald F. Kendrick of Middle Tennessee State University, Thomas Nygren of Ohio State University, and Faye Plascak-Craig of Marian College.

*Lee A. Kirkpatrick*
*Brooke C. Feeney*

## About SPSS/PC+ Versions 4.0 and 5.0

The two most recent versions of SPSS/PC+ for DOS, Versions 4.0 and 5.0, are very similar or identical in most respects. Most procedures work exactly the same in both versions and produce identical outputs. Thus, with just a few exceptions, the user need not be concerned about which version he or she is using. As far as the material covered in this manual is concerned, the only differences between the two versions are the following:

1. In Version 5.0, an alternative method for entering data was added to the program. Called **QED,** this new module allows you to enter data using a spreadsheet-like interface rather than the procedure explained in this manual (i.e., use of **DATA LIST, BEGIN DATA,** and **END DATA**). Although the spreadsheet approach to data entry seems like a good idea in principle, in practice we believe that for most students it proves to be more trouble than it is worth. Thus, we have chosen not to cover **QED** in this manual. The method of data entry described in the manual will work identically in both Versions 4.0 and 5.0.

2. One procedure covered in this manual, **T-TEST,** produces output that is arranged and labeled rather differently in Versions 4.0 and 5.0. The actual information provided varies little between the versions, but the superficial differences in format can be confusing. For this procedure (and only this one), we therefore have included separate sample outputs (and corresponding annotations) for Versions 4.0 and 5.0. For all other procedures discussed in the manual, the two versions produce identical outputs.

3. One other procedure covered in this manual, **CORRELATIONS,** differs in one subtle but important way between Versions 4.0 and 5.0. In Version 4.0, **CORRELATIONS** prints the results of *one-tailed* significance tests by default. To obtain two-tailed tests, one needs to specify the subcommand **OPTIONS 3.** This default has been changed in Version 5.0, so that unless specified otherwise, SPSS/PC+ produces *two-tailed* significance tests (**OPTION 3** now produces one-tailed tests). In our opinion, this change is welcome and long overdue, but it could easily prove confusing to the novice user. Whichever version you are using, examine your output carefully and you will find a note indicating whether the *p*-values printed refer to one-tailed or two-tailed probabilities.

# *A Simple Guide to SPSS/PC+®*

*For Versions 4.0 and 5.0*

# Introduction to SPSS/PC+

## Overview

To analyze data with SPSS/PC+ you need to know two things. First, you need to speak the same language that SPSS/PC+ does in order to tell it what you want it to do. SPSS/PC+ doesn't speak English, so you essentially have to learn a new language to communicate with it. Fortunately, "SPSSese" is related to English and uses many English words and phrases, so it isn't as difficult to learn as some other computer programming languages that bear little resemblance to English (or any other spoken language). Following this introductory section, the remainder of this manual can be thought of as a kind of phrase book in which you can look up the SPSSese phrase for statements like "calculate the correlation between this set of SAT scores and this set of IQ scores." It's a little like going to Paris and using your phrase book to figure out how to ask someone, in French, where the bathroom is.

The other thing you need to know is how to interact with SPSS/PC+ in the first place—that is, how to convey these SPSSese messages to it. Obviously this involves typing at a keyboard rather than speaking aloud (although someday this may well change!). This is like trying to send a letter or electronic mail message to someone in France; not only do you need to know French, but also you need to know how to address and seal an envelope, how to put the proper postage on it, and where the post office is. Moreover, you need to know how to get the reply you receive—i.e., where your mailbox is and how to open it. This introductory section provides an overview of how to accomplish these things.

## Starting Up SPSS/PC+

The SPSS/PC+ program is started in different ways depending on your installation. On many computer networks, such as those in computer labs at many colleges and universities, the program is listed in a menu along with a variety of other statistical programs. In this case, use the arrow keys to locate the program name in the menu system and hit the ENTER key to enter the program. (On some systems you might be prompted to enter some optional "parameters" at this point; if so, just hit the ENTER key again.) If you are using the program on a computer that is not linked to a network file server, then the program usually can be started by merely typing the program name "SPSSPC" at the DOS prompt, perhaps after selecting the appropriate directory.

The SPSS/PC+ screen that will appear is divided into three major sections. The top half of the screen contains (1) the Menu window (on the left) and (2) the Help window (on the right). The bottom half of the screen contains (3) an Edit window (usually blue on color monitors) with a blinking square cursor.

## *Entering Commands into SPSS/PC+*

Although there are several ways to interact with SPSS/PC+, this manual will focus on just one for the sake of simplicity. Later on, when you feel more comfortable with the program, you might want to explore some of the other options on your own. However, all of the options follow the basic procedure described here.

1. First, commands written in SPSSese are somehow written or assembled in the Edit window at the bottom of the SPSS/PC+ screen. This can be done in several ways, as explained later, but ultimately the idea is for the blue window to contain a list of commands written in the correct order for execution. These commands include information about what the data represent and how they are structured, the data themselves, and instructions for the analyses you wish to conduct on those data. As noted earlier, most of this manual is concerned with the content of these commands—what they should say and how they should say it.

2. An Edit window full of commands is like a letter that hasn't yet been put in the mailbox. Once your commands have been recorded in the Edit window, they need to be executed. When the commands are executed, SPSS/PC+ will begin generating output from the specified procedures. The "output" produced by the program—that is, your results—will be displayed on your computer screen. You may write down the critical information from your output at this time.

3. You may also want a more permanent copy of the output. At the same time your results are being displayed on the screen, an identical copy of the output is being stored on the computer in a file. You will want to know how to find this file, possibly edit it (to make it prettier or to delete unwanted information), and print or copy it to your floppy disk.

4. Eventually, you will need to know how to exit the program so you can go home.

Each of these steps is described in greater detail in the following sections.

## *1. Entering Commands into the Edit Window*

There are actually three ways to enter commands into the Edit window:

a. You can build commands by selecting items from the Menu window (top left of screen) and "pasting" them into the Edit window. We believe that for most users this can be a cumbersome and confusing procedure, and we recommend against it for this reason.

b. You can, in advance, write out all your SPSS/PC+ commands in a file, using a word processor or other text editor. Then, once you're in SPSS/PC+, you can use a special command to call that file into the Edit window. Because this too can be complicated, we recommend against using this method in the beginning. Besides, this procedure is really useful only when you have very large and complex sets of SPSS/PC+ commands, which for present purposes we assume is not the case. If you're interested in this method, see Appendix A for instructions on how to do it.

c. Finally, and most simply, you can type your commands into the Edit window directly. The Edit window is itself a kind of word processor or text editor (though not a particularly good one). This is the procedure we recommend and explain in this manual.

When you first enter SPSS/PC+, you will see a blinking *square* cursor in the top left corner of the Edit window, which indicates that you are in the "Menu mode." If you try to type something, you'll find that it doesn't work; at most, some weird things will happen in the Menu window in the upper left corner of the screen. What you *can* do in this mode, however, is use the up and down arrow keys to move the cursor around the Menu window. This mode is used for entering SPSS/PC+ commands in the first way we described. As noted above, we recommend against this. Read on to see what you should do instead.

In order to type commands directly onto the Edit screen, you must first press ALT-E. (*Note:* This means to press the ALT key and, while holding it down, hit and release the E key. Then release the ALT key.) Once you have done this, the square cursor should change to a little *line* cursor, which indicates that you are in the "Edit mode." You are now "in" the Edit window rather than the Menu window. You are ready to begin typing your commands.

Now, turn to the appropriate section of the manual for the analysis you wish to perform. The following sections provide sample problems, data analyses, and interpretations for statistical procedures that are generally covered in introductory psychological statistics courses.

For editing commands, the Edit window works very much like a simple word-processing program. A "simple" word processor is adequate for current purposes, though. You don't need to do any fancy formatting; you just need to type in some commands. Although this editor does have some fairly advanced features, you probably won't need them and we won't bother to explain them. You can probably fix your typos and do other minor editing by using a few simple functions that work just the way you'd expect them to: (1) the up, down, left, and right arrow keys move the cursor around the screen; (2) the Delete or DEL key deletes the character on which the cursor is located; and (3) the Insert or INS key toggles back and forth between "insert" and "overwrite" modes. Just experiment a little and you'll see how easy it is.

## *2. Executing SPSS/PC+ Commands*

Once all of your commands have been typed into the Edit window, you are ready to "run" or execute the commands. Although you can see the list of commands in front of you, SPSS/PC+ doesn't actually do any computations until you tell it to do so.

Use the arrow keys to place the cursor somewhere on the *first* command that you wish to execute (probably the top line), press F10, and then press ENTER. SPSS/PC+ will execute the command on which the cursor lies plus all commands after it, until it runs out of commands or until it encounters an error.

Your analysis should run and display your output on the screen. Whenever you see a *MORE* prompt at the top right side of the screen, press the spacebar to move to the next screen(s) of your results. Continue to press the spacebar as directed until you are back to the original screen with the menus and Edit screen.

If your analysis does not run, you may see the word *Error* followed by suggestions (albeit cryptic ones, usually) about what may be wrong with your commands. In this case, you will also continue to press the spacebar until you are back to the original screen. Check your commands carefully, make any necessary repairs (using the editing functions described above), and reexecute the analysis by again moving the cursor to the top line of commands and pressing F10. If the program correctly executed several commands before encountering an error, it usually isn't necessary to reexecute those commands that ran properly. Instead, you can just move the cursor to the line on which the error occurred and start executing (F10) at this point. On the other hand, there is no harm in starting at the beginning again, on your first command line, and we recommend this just to be on the safe side. If you've followed the manual carefully, you probably just forgot a period, misspelled a word, or made some other simple mistake. Don't panic.

After you execute a command or commands and you have viewed the output on the screen, SPSS/PC+ will automatically put you back into the Menu mode, as you were when you started the program. That is, you will have a square cursor in the Edit window again and typing will be fruitless. Press ALT-E to switch back to the Edit mode if you wish to edit or type in more commands. (Remember, any time you find yourself in the Menu mode—that is, typing does not result in anything happening in the Edit screen—just hit ALT-E to switch back to the Edit mode.)

*An Alternative.* We have suggested typing in all of your SPSS/PC+ commands at once and then executing them together. However, an alternative is to execute your commands one at a time. That is, you can type in your first command, then execute it (using F10 and ENTER), then type in the next command and execute it, and so on. It doesn't matter to SPSS/PC+, so do it whichever way you prefer.

### *3. Accessing the Output from Your Data Analyses*

At the same time your output is being displayed on your screen, it is also being saved in a file (on your hard drive) called *SPSS.LIS*. (This file is in a format called "ASCII" or a "DOS file," in case that means anything to you. If not, don't worry about it.) You can access this file by using the DOS Editor, WordPerfect, or any other word-processing or text-editing program you wish. After exiting SPSS/PC+ (described next), just call the file *SPSS.LIS* into the editor and revise it as desired, just as you would any other paper or document. For example, you might want to change the margins or font or delete material that you don't want or need. Finally, save a copy of the revised version on your floppy disk and print it.

One problem you might have is locating this file on the hard disk. On a stand-alone desktop computer, *SPSS.LIS* is usually found in the same directory on the hard drive that contains the SPSS/PC+ program. In computer labs shared by many people, SPSS/PC+ might be set up to save the output file in some other directory. If you can't find it, get help from your local computer guru.

The other problem you might have is that once you call *SPSS.LIS* into your word processor or text editor, you discover that the file created by SPSS/PC+ is too wide (that is, there are more characters on some lines than will fit on the screen or a printed page) and as a result some lines "wrap" around on the screen. You can go ahead and print the file this way, but it will look messy and it may foul up the formatting of tables and other parts of the output. We recommend you fix this by either changing the font (that is, have the word processor and printer use smaller letters so it can fit more on each line) or reducing the size of the margins so everything fits on a line. Experiment and find a procedure that works for you on the computer you typically use, and make a note of it for future reference.

### *4. Exiting SPSS/PC+*

Once you have finished analyzing your data and are ready to exit SPSS/PC+, type and execute the command **FINISH.** This may seem like an odd way to exit the program, but trust us. Type the command **FINISH** into the Edit window just as you would type any other SPSS/PC+ command, and execute the command by moving the cursor to that line and pressing F10. This will take you out of SPSS/PC+ and bring you back to the DOS prompt or menu system.

## *Some General Notes on SPSS/PC+ Commands*

If you follow our examples carefully and don't improvise too much, you shouldn't have many problems. However, a few general features of SPSS/PC+ commands are worth knowing.

1. All SPSS/PC+ commands should begin in the first column (that is, don't indent them), and all must end with a *period* (.). If you ever get an error message from SPSS/PC+, the first thing to look for is whether you left out a period at the end of a command. No matter what error message SPSS/PC+ displays, a missing period may very well be the culprit—even though the message will not say anything like "missing period." This is a very easy mistake to make and, believe us, we both do it all the time.

2. Between the beginning of the command and the final period, there is usually a great deal of flexibility in format. For example, wherever a space is required (between words, for example), you can always use two or more spaces if you prefer. This allows you considerable freedom in writing your commands in a way that is easily readable, aesthetically pleasing to you, or whatever. In addition, commas and spaces are usually interchangeable.

3. If a command is too long to fit on one line, there is no problem. Just hit ENTER at some point to move to the next line and continue typing the command. Use as many lines as you need: SPSS/PC+ will just keep reading until it finds a period (don't forget that period!) signaling the end of the command. These "continuation" lines do *not* have to begin in the first column; in fact, we personally prefer to indent continuation lines a few spaces

to help make the program look nice and enhance readability. *Important note:* If you do indent lines, do so using the spacebar rather than TAB.

4. As will become apparent, many SPSS/PC+ commands include one or more subcommands that specify details of the analysis. Subcommands are usually separated from each other with slashes (/). (*Note:* These are "forward" slashes, not backslashes.) Because subcommands are just part of the same command, it doesn't matter if you put extra spaces between them, if you begin subcommands on a new line, or if you have other variations. Again, we sometimes like to start a new (indented) line for each subcommand for aesthetic purposes, but this is by no means necessary.

## *On the Remainder of the Manual*

The remainder of this manual presents examples of the SPSS/PC+ commands needed to run different kinds of statistical analyses and illustrates the output generated by these procedures. We have followed two conventions (as consistently as possible) in presenting this material: (1) all commands and data input (on the problem analysis sheets) that must be typed directly into SPSS/PC+ are in **bold print**, and (2) the output that is produced by SPSS/PC+ appears in `computer type`. Variable names and data are specific to the particular sample problems only; you will of course substitute your own data and your own variable names for those in the examples.

• • • • • •

# *Getting SPSS/PC+ to Read Your Data: The **DATA LIST** Command*

When you enter SPSS/PC+ to analyze some data, the first thing you always need to do is type in your data and tell SPSS/PC+ what the data represent. This is accomplished using (1) the **DATA LIST** command, which tells SPSS/PC+ how to read the data, and (2) the data themselves, sandwiched between a **BEGIN DATA** command and an **END DATA** command.

Here's an example:

```
DATA LIST FIXED / STUDENT 1-2 GENDER 4 SCORE 6-7.
BEGIN DATA.
 1 1 87
 2 1 53
 3 1 92
 4 1 70
 5 1 78
 6 1 73
 7 1 91
 8 1 60
 9 1 77
10 1 82
11 1 85
12 1 33
13 1 88
14 1 98
15 1 88
16 2 89
17 2 73
18 2 91
19 2 76
20 2 75
21 2 89
22 2 81
23 2 83
24 2 68
25 2 86
26 2 55
```

```
27 2 89
28 2 89
29 2 70
30 2 93
END DATA.
```

The **DATA LIST** command is used to define the data that you are going to analyze. This command designates the variable names and the format in which the data are entered. Every SPSS/PC+ job begins with a **DATA LIST** command because the program obviously needs to read the relevant data before it can analyze them. (There are sometimes alternatives to this, however; see Appendix B if you're interested in some more advanced techniques.)

The subcommand **FIXED** indicates that your data will be defined in a "fixed format." This simply means that the data are arranged in exactly the same way on every line. (An alternative, **FREE** format, does not require that the data be lined up neatly in columns. We advise against this, however. We think it is good practice to keep your data neatly arranged in columns so it is easier to detect data-entry errors in the raw data by visual inspection.)

In our example the first variable name specified in the **DATA LIST** command is **STUDENT**, which is just an identification number for each case. (Usually it is not essential to include an identification variable, but it is good practice to do so anyway.) The numerical values for this variable occupy positions 1 and 2 on each record. The second variable name specified in the **DATA LIST** command is **GENDER**, and the data for this variable occupy position 4 on each line of data. **SCORE** is the third variable name specified in the **DATA LIST** command, and it appears in positions 6 and 7 of each data line.

*Naming Variables.* STUDENT, GENDER, and SCORE are names that were chosen to describe the variables for this particular problem. You will use different names more appropriate to your own problem. In choosing variable names, note that they must be no more than eight characters in length. They can be any combination of letters and numbers. Usually you'll want to use words or abbreviations that will help you to remember what the variable names mean. For example, the meaning of "GENDER" is obvious, although we could just as well have used "SEX" or "ACIJD5" had we wanted to.

*Data Format.* You have a great deal of flexibility in choosing a format for the data. In this example, we entered the data leaving a blank space between the variables on each line; notice that columns 3 and 5 are always empty. This is purely for aesthetic purposes; it makes it easier to eyeball the data to make sure everything is lined up properly. However, you may include more spaces, or no spaces, between variables if you prefer. The only thing that is critical is that you write your **DATA LIST** command to conform precisely to the format in which the data are entered.

It is important to determine in advance how many columns you will need for each variable. Generally this will be the number of columns required by the largest value you will be entering for that variable. For example, a variable that represents subjects' ages will require two columns (for two digits) unless every subject is less than 10 years old (in which case one column would suffice) or unless you have one or more subjects over age 99 (in which case you'll need three columns). If some of the values do not require as many columns as you have allocated for that variable, it is usually best to "right justify" the value by putting either a blank space or zero before, rather than after, the digit(s) to be entered. For example, suppose someone in the data set above had a score of 7—a one-digit number. For that subject, enter the score as "07" (zero seven) or as " 7" ([space] seven), rather than as "7 " (seven [space]).

*Decimals.* If any of your data include decimals, there are two ways that these values can be read into SPSS/PC+. You may choose whichever method you prefer. The most straightforward way is simply to enter the data (between the **BEGIN DATA** and **END DATA** commands) including the decimal points. If you do this, however, remember that the decimal point itself takes up a column on each data line (just as another digit would) and the **DATA LIST** command must accurately reflect this. For example, if your data on a variable include values such as 2.35 and 4.00, you need to specify four columns for the variable on the **DATA LIST** command (e.g., 1–4 or 5–8).

Alternatively, if you plan to type in the same number of decimal places for each subject, you can omit the decimal points when typing in your data and let SPSS/PC+ insert them for you. (This is especially helpful if you have a large amount of data to enter because typing the decimal points can get to be a nuisance.) In the **DATA LIST** command, after the name and column numbers of the variable, simply type within parentheses the number of decimal places you wish to define for that variable. This method is demonstrated in the **DATA LIST** command in the example for simple regression (see page 71). The data for that sample problem include grade point averages for a sample of school children. We omitted the decimal points when entering the data and just typed in values of 212, 300, 400, and so on. In the **DATA LIST** command, we told SPSS/PC+ that the values for our variable **GPA** occupy positions **7–9** on each line of data. (*Note:* Only three columns are needed with the decimal points being left out.) Next, we typed **(2)** to tell SPSS/PC+ that there are two decimal places for this variable. When SPSS/PC+ reads the data, it internally does the calculations to insert the decimal points. You won't actually see anything change on the screen, but if you ask SPSS/PC+ to calculate the values for this variable, you'll see that the decimals have been handled correctly.

The commands **BEGIN DATA** and **END DATA** are used to indicate the beginning and ending of your actual data. Your data should be typed between these commands in the format specified in the **DATA LIST** command. Each line contains the data for one subject. (Another way of doing this, in which the data are stored in a separate file, is explained in Appendix A. For simple problems, however, the method described here is much easier.)

After the **END DATA** command, you are ready to type in one or more commands to run analyses on your data, as explained in the remainder of this manual. Note that once the data have been read—that is, the **DATA LIST** command has been executed—you can run as many procedures as you wish without reexecuting the **DATA LIST** command.

# Frequency Distributions and Descriptive Statistics

## Sample Problem

Fifteen men and fifteen women in an introductory psychological statistics course have taken their midterm exams. Their scores are listed in the table.

| *Student* | *Gender** | *Score* |
|---|---|---|
| 1 | 1 | 87 |
| 2 | 1 | 53 |
| 3 | 1 | 92 |
| 4 | 1 | 70 |
| 5 | 1 | 78 |
| 6 | 1 | 73 |
| 7 | 1 | 91 |
| 8 | 1 | 60 |
| 9 | 1 | 77 |
| 10 | 1 | 82 |
| 11 | 1 | 85 |
| 12 | 1 | 33 |
| 13 | 1 | 88 |
| 14 | 1 | 98 |
| 15 | 1 | 88 |
| 16 | 2 | 89 |
| 17 | 2 | 73 |
| 18 | 2 | 91 |
| 19 | 2 | 76 |
| 20 | 2 | 75 |
| 21 | 2 | 89 |
| 22 | 2 | 81 |
| 23 | 2 | 83 |
| 24 | 2 | 68 |
| 25 | 2 | 86 |
| 26 | 2 | 55 |
| 27 | 2 | 89 |
| 28 | 2 | 89 |
| 29 | 2 | 70 |
| 30 | 2 | 93 |

*For gender: 1 = male, 2 = female.

## *Analysis: Frequency Distributions*

```
DATA LIST FIXED / STUDENT 1-2 GENDER 4 SCORE 6-7.
BEGIN DATA.
 1 1 87
 2 1 53
 3 1 92
 4 1 70
 5 1 78
 6 1 73
 7 1 91
 8 1 60
 9 1 77
10 1 82
11 1 85
12 1 33
13 1 88
14 1 98
15 1 88
16 2 89
17 2 73
18 2 91
19 2 76
20 2 75
21 2 89
22 2 81
23 2 83
24 2 68
25 2 86
26 2 55
27 2 89
28 2 89
29 2 70
30 2 93
END DATA.
FREQUENCIES /VARIABLES GENDER SCORE /STATISTICS ALL.
```

The **FREQUENCIES** command tells SPSS/PC+ to produce frequency distributions. The subcommand **/VARIABLES** specifies the variables for which you would like SPSS/PC+ to produce a frequency distribution, in this case **GENDER** and **SCORE**.

Alternatively, you can write **/VARIABLES ALL**, replacing the list of variable names with the word **ALL**. This tells SPSS/PC+ to create a frequency distribution for every variable it knows about.

The subcommand **/STATISTICS ALL** tells SPSS/PC+ to produce all available summary statistics for the variables **GENDER** and **SCORE** (listed on the **/VARIABLES** subcommand). (If you want only certain statistics, you'll need to consult a manual to determine how to replace **ALL** with the names of specific statistics. Usually, however, it's easier to just ask for all statistics and then ignore the ones in which you're not interested.)

The following output is from the sample program.

```
. . . . . . . . . . . . . . . . . . . . . . . . . . . . . . . . . . . . . . . . . . . . .

GENDER

                                                                Valid       Cum
Value Label                       Value  Frequency  Percent  Percent  Percent

                                      1         15     50.0     50.0     50.0
                                      2         15     50.0     50.0    100.0
                                          -------  -------  -------
                                  Total         30    100.0    100.0

. . . . . . . . . . . . . . . . . . . . . . . . . . . . . . . . . . . . . . . . . . . . .

GENDER

Mean           1.500     Std err        .093     Median         1.500
Mode           1.000     Std dev        .509     Variance        .259
Kurtosis      -2.148     S E Kurt       .833     Skewness        .000
S E Skew        .427     Range         1.000     Minimum        1.000
Maximum        2.000     Sum          45.000

* Multiple modes exist.  The smallest value is shown.

Valid cases       30     Missing cases       0

. . . . . . . . . . . . . . . . . . . . . . . . . . . . . . . . . . . . . . . . . . . . .
```

SCORE

| Value Label | Value | Frequency | Percent | Valid Percent | Cum Percent |
|---|---|---|---|---|---|
| | 33 | 1 | 3.3 | 3.3 | 3.3 |
| | 53 | 1 | 3.3 | 3.3 | 6.7 |
| | 55 | 1 | 3.3 | 3.3 | 10.0 |
| | 60 | 1 | 3.3 | 3.3 | 13.3 |
| | 68 | 1 | 3.3 | 3.3 | 16.7 |
| | 70 | 2 | 6.7 | 6.7 | 23.3 |
| | 73 | 2 | 6.7 | 6.7 | 30.0 |
| | 75 | 1 | 3.3 | 3.3 | 33.3 |
| | 76 | 1 | 3.3 | 3.3 | 36.7 |
| | 77 | 1 | 3.3 | 3.3 | 40.0 |
| | 78 | 1 | 3.3 | 3.3 | 43.3 |
| | 81 | 1 | 3.3 | 3.3 | 46.7 |
| | 82 | 1 | 3.3 | 3.3 | 50.0 |
| | 83 | 1 | 3.3 | 3.3 | 53.3 |
| | 85 | 1 | 3.3 | 3.3 | 56.7 |
| | 86 | 1 | 3.3 | 3.3 | 60.0 |
| | 87 | 1 | 3.3 | 3.3 | 63.3 |
| | 88 | 2 | 6.7 | 6.7 | 70.0 |
| | 89 | 4 | 13.3 | 13.3 | 83.3 |
| | 91 | 2 | 6.7 | 6.7 | 90.0 |
| | 92 | 1 | 3.3 | 3.3 | 93.3 |
| | 93 | 1 | 3.3 | 3.3 | 96.7 |
| | 98 | 1 | 3.3 | 3.3 | 100.0 |
| | Total | 30 | 100.0 | 100.0 | |

SCORE

| | | | | | |
|---|---|---|---|---|---|
| Mean | 78.733 | Std err | 2.597 | Median | 82.500 |
| Mode | 89.000 | Std dev | 14.222 | Variance | 202.271 |
| Kurtosis | 2.474 | S E Kurt | .833 | Skewness | -1.443 |
| S E Skew | .427 | Range | 65.000 | Minimum | 33.000 |
| Maximum | 98.000 | Sum | 2362.000 | | |

Valid cases 30 Missing cases 0

In the frequency distributions, the first column ("Value") lists all values that were found on the variable; the second column ("Frequency") lists the number of cases that have that value; the third column ("Percent") is the percentage of all cases that have this value (i.e., the frequency divided by the total number of cases); the fourth column ("Valid Percent") is the percentage of all "valid" cases—that is, the cases that were not missing data on this variable—that have that value; and the fifth column ("Cum Percent") lists the cumulative percentage for that value—that is, the percent of valid cases that have this value or less. Note that "Percent" and "Valid Percent" will be identical if there are no missing values on this variable. The number of valid cases and the number of missing cases are given at the bottom of the table.

Some of these statistics, such as kurtosis and skew (and their standard errors), are somewhat esoteric and are probably not of interest to you. The more familiar statistics are the mean, median, mode, variance, standard deviation, and standard error.

It is important to note that the variance and standard deviation are based on the variance-estimate formulas, in which the numerator is divided by $N - 1$ instead of by $N$.

## *Analysis: Histograms*

The **FREQUENCIES** command can also be used to produce a histogram or a bar chart. To do so, use the following **FREQUENCIES** command in place of the previous one.

```
FREQUENCIES /VARIABLES SCORE /FORMAT NOTABLE /HISTOGRAM.
```

The **/HISTOGRAM** subcommand tells SPSS/PC+ to produce histograms. The **/VARIABLES** subcommand again specifies the variable(s) for which histograms are desired.

The subcommand **/FORMAT NOTABLE** tells SPSS/PC+ to suppress the frequency distribution (as illustrated in the preceding output) that would otherwise be produced for the variable(s) by the **FREQUENCIES** command.

If you wish to produce a bar chart instead of a histogram, replace the subcommand **/HISTOGRAM** with the subcommand **/BARCHART**.

The following output is from the **FREQUENCIES** command given here. Output for **/BARCHART** is not illustrated.

SCORE

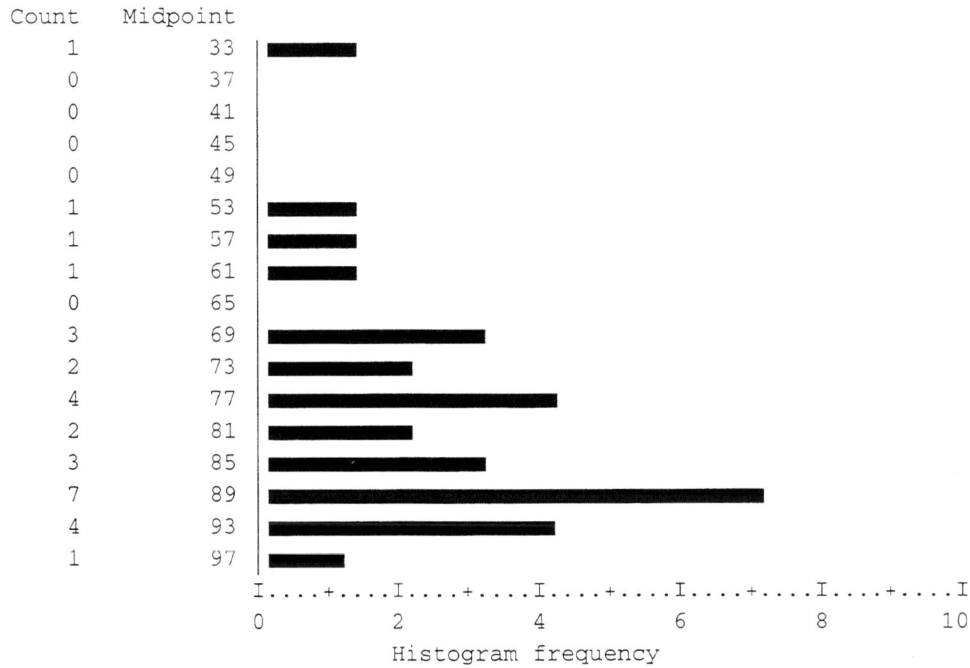


SCORE

```
Valid cases        30        Missing cases        0
```

## *Analysis: Stem-and-Leaf Displays*

The **EXAMINE** command is used to produce stem-and-leaf plots.

```
EXAMINE /VARIABLES SCORE /PLOT STEMLEAF.
```

This command line tells SPSS/PC+ to produce a stem-and-leaf plot (**/PLOT STEMLEAF**) for the variable **SCORE**. A variety of descriptive statistics are also produced by default.

```
. . . . . . . . . . . . . . . . . . . . . . . . . . . . . . . . . . . . . . . . . . . .

    SCORE

Valid cases:    30.0  Missing cases:   0    Percent missing:    .0


Mean    78.7333 Std Err  2.5966 Min           33.0000 Skewness -1.4428
Median  82.5000 Variance 202.2713 Max 98.0000  S E Skew  .4269
5% Trim 79.9259 Std Dev  14.2222 Range 65.0000 Kurtosis 2.4739
                IQR 16.7500 S E Kurt  .8327

. . . . . . . . . . . . . . . . . . . . . . . . . . . . . . . . . . . . . . . . . . . .

    SCORE

  Frequency    Stem &  Leaf

     1.00 Extremes     (33)
     1.00        5  *  3
     1.00        5  .  5
     1.00        6  *  0
     1.00        6  .  8
     4.00        7  *  0033
     4.00        7  .  5678
     3.00        8  *  123
     9.00        8  .  567889999
     4.00        9  *  1123
     1.00        9  .  8

 Stem width:  10
 Each leaf:        1 case(s)

. . . . . . . . . . . . . . . . . . . . . . . . . . . . . . . . . . . . . . . . . . . .
```

## *Analysis: Descriptive Statistics*

The **DESCRIPTIVES** command is used to produce univariate descriptive statistics, such as means and variances. Although most of the same statistics can be obtained with the **FREQUENCIES** or **EXAMINE** commands shown previously, **DESCRIPTIVES** formats the results in a way that is sometimes more convenient, particularly if you have a large number of variables.

```
DESCRIPTIVES /VARIABLES GENDER SCORE /STATISTICS ALL.
```

This command line tells SPSS/PC+ to produce all available descriptive statistics for the variables GENDER and SCORE.

*Note:* The median and mode are not among the statistics available from the **DESCRIPTIVES** command. The **FREQUENCIES** command must be used to produce the median and mode.

The following output is from the command given here.

```
. . . . . . . . . . . . . . . . . . . . . . . . . . . . . . . . . . . . . . . . . . . . .

Number of Valid Observations (Listwise) =        30.00

Variable  GENDER

Mean              1.500              S.E. Mean          .093
Std Dev            .509              Variance           .259
Kurtosis         -2.148              S.E. Kurt          .833
Skewness           .000              S.E. Skew          .427
Range             1.000              Minimum               1
Maximum               2              Sum              45.000

Valid Observations          30      Missing Observations -        0

. . . . . . . . . . . . . . . . . . . . . . . . . . . . . . . . . . . . . . . . . . . . .

Number of Valid Observations (Listwise) =        30.00

Variable  SCORE

Mean             78.733              S.E. Mean         2.597
Std Dev          14.222              Variance        202.271
Kurtosis          2.474              S.E. Kurt          .833
Skewness         -1.443              S.E. Skew          .427
Range            65.000              Minimum              33
Maximum              98              Sum            2362.000

Valid Observations -        30      Missing Observations -        0

. . . . . . . . . . . . . . . . . . . . . . . . . . . . . . . . . . . . . . . . . . . . .
```

# One-Sample t-Test

## Sample Problem

The superintendent of the Riverwalk School District claims that the students in his district are more intelligent, on the average, than the general population of students. The mean IQ of the general population of schoolchildren is 105. A study was conducted to determine the IQs of a sample of schoolchildren in the Riverwalk District. The results are listed in the table.

| *Student* | *IQ Score* |
|---|---|
| 1 | 110 |
| 2 | 105 |
| 3 | 102 |
| 4 | 112 |
| 5 | 120 |
| 6 | 107 |
| 7 | 99 |
| 8 | 100 |
| 9 | 109 |
| 10 | 103 |
| 11 | 115 |
| 12 | 125 |
| 13 | 115 |
| 14 | 106 |
| 15 | 110 |
| 16 | 110 |
| 17 | 117 |
| 18 | 98 |
| 19 | 124 |
| 20 | 107 |
| 21 | 112 |
| 22 | 122 |
| 23 | 104 |
| 24 | 105 |
| 25 | 110 |
| 26 | 120 |
| 27 | 125 |
| 28 | 120 |
| 29 | 100 |
| 30 | 110 |

In this problem, we are testing the null hypothesis that the mean IQ of all children in the Riverwalk School District equals 105, and this will be assessed by examining a random sample of Riverwalk students. This value was selected because it is already known that 105 is the overall mean IQ of all students in all school districts. We want to know whether the Riverwalk population is any different. Is the mean of this sample "significantly" different from 105?

## *Analysis*

```
DATA LIST FIXED / STUDENT 1-2 IQ 4-6.
BEGIN DATA.
 1 110
 2 105
 3 102
 4 112
 5 120
 6 107
 7  99
 8 100
 9 109
10 103
11 115
12 125
13 115
14 106
15 110
16 110
17 117
18  98
19 124
20 107
21 112
22 122
23 104
24 105
25 110
26 120
27 125
28 120
```

```
29 100
30 110
END DATA.
COMPUTE CONSTANT = 105.
T-TEST /PAIRS IQ CONSTANT.
```

SPSS/PC+ does not contain a specific program for calculating a single-sample *t*-test. Therefore, it must be "tricked" into conducting this type of *t*-test with a program designed for "paired" or "matched pairs" *t*-tests. (The more common application of the paired *t*-test command is illustrated in a subsequent section.)

This test is done in SPSS/PC+ with the **COMPUTE CONSTANT = 105** command. This **COMPUTE** command tells SPSS/PC+ to create a new variable called "CONSTANT" (or any other name you might assign to it) and to give each subject a score of 105 on that variable. (The **COMPUTE** command is very useful for many other purposes, too; see Appendix C for more information.)

The subcommand **/PAIRS IQ CONSTANT** tells SPSS/PC+ to test whether the means of the two variables, IQ and CONSTANT, are equal. This may seem odd given that CONSTANT isn't really a variable (it doesn't vary), but trust us, this is how to do the test in SPSS/PC+.

*Important note:* Because the output from the **T-TEST** procedure looks very different in SPSS/PC+ Versions 4.0 and 5.0, both are displayed in this section.

*Annotated Output for Version 4:*

```
. . . . . . . . . . . . . . . . . . . . . . . . . . . . . . . . . . . . . . . . . . . . .

Paired samples t-test:  IQ
                        CONSTANT

Variable     Number                  Standard   Standard
            of Cases     Mean       Deviation     Error

IQ              30     110.7333       8.051       1.470
CONSTANT        30     105.0000        .000        .000

                                   |                   |
(Difference) Standard  Standard    |         2-Tail    |    t    Degrees of   2-Tail
    Mean    Deviation    Error     |  Corr.  Prob.     |  Value    Freedom     Prob.
                                   |                   |
   5.7333       8.051    1.470          .       .          3.90       29        .001

. . . . . . . . . . . . . . . . . . . . . . . . . . . . . . . . . . . . . . . . . . . . .
```

When you execute the **COMPUTE** and **T-TEST** commands, SPSS/PC+ produces some descriptive statistics—such as number of cases, mean, standard deviation, and standard error—for the variables IQ (IQs for our sample of Riverwalk students) and CONSTANT, which we created with the **COMPUTE** command. Note that the standard deviation for CONSTANT is zero: Remember, everyone has the same score on this variable (105), so it has no variance in this case. Of primary interest to us are the mean (110.7333) and standard deviation (8.051) of IQs for the Riverwalk sample.

Beneath the descriptive statistics for each sample, SPSS/PC+ reports the results of the significance test. "(Difference) Mean" is the difference between the observed sample mean (110.7333) and the hypothesized mean (105). (Note that if the sample mean had been less than 105, the difference mean would be reported as a negative number.) The "Standard Deviation" and "Standard Error" that follow refer to difference scores, computed by subtracting 105 from each student's IQ. In the one-sample test, these values correspond exactly to the standard deviation and standard error for the Riverwalk sample.

To the right of these values are the results of the *t*-test itself. The degrees of freedom (sample size minus one) and the two-tailed probability value ("*p*-value") are also computed. The result is considered statistically significant if the *p*-value is less than the chosen alpha level, usually .05 or .01. In this case, *p* is definitely less than .05 (and .01), so the result is considered statistically significant and the null hypothesis is rejected.

If you were doing the problem by hand, you would use a table in your statistics textbook to determine the critical *t*-value associated with 29 degrees of freedom—this value is 3.659 (for alpha = .05)—and then compare the observed *t*-value to the critical value. The observed *t*-value (3.90) is greater than the critical *t*-value, so you would reject the null hypothesis.

Note that the output from most statistical procedures in SPSS/PC+ works this same way. That is, SPSS/PC+ usually prints the *p*-value associated with the test statistic, and it is up to you to decide whether *p* is sufficiently small to reject the null hypothesis (that is, whether *p* is smaller than your chosen alpha). Both methods—comparing critical and observed *t*-values and comparing critical (alpha) and observed (*p*) probabilities—will lead to the same conclusion for any given problem.

*Annotated Output for Version 5:*

```
. . . . . . . . . . . . . . . . . . . . . . . . . . . . . . . . . . . . . . . .

                    - - - t-tests for paired samples - - -

                    Number of          2-tail
  Variable            pairs     Corr    Sig         Mean       SD    SE of Mean
 ------------------------------------------------------------------------------
  IQ                                              110.7333     8.051      1.470
                       30         .       .
  CONSTANT                                        105.0000      .000       .000
 ------------------------------------------------------------------------------

               Paired Differences              |
  Mean          SD          SE of Mean         |    t-value     df   2-tail Sig
 ------------------------------------------------------------------------------
  5.7333        8.051         1.470            |      3.90      29        .001
 95% CI (2.726, 8.740)                         |

. . . . . . . . . . . . . . . . . . . . . . . . . . . . . . . . . . . . . . . .
```

When you execute the **COMPUTE** and **T-TEST** commands, SPSS/PC+ produces some descriptive statistics (number of cases, mean, standard deviation, and standard error) for the variables IQ (IQs for our sample of Riverwalk students) and CONSTANT (which we created with the **COMPUTE** command). Note that the standard deviation ("SD") for CONSTANT is zero. Remember, everyone has the same score on this variable (105), so it has no variance in this case. Of primary interest to us are the mean (110.7333) and standard deviation (8.051) of IQs for the Riverwalk sample.

Beneath the descriptive statistics for each sample, SPSS/PC+ reports the results of the significance test. "Mean" under "Paired Differences" is the difference between the observed sample mean (110.7333) and the hypothesized mean (105). (Note that if the sample mean had been less than 105, the difference mean would be reported as a negative number.) The standard deviation ("SD") and standard error ("SE of Mean") that follow refer to difference scores, computed by subtracting 105 from each student's IQ. In the one-sample test, these values correspond exactly to the standard deviation and standard error for the Riverwalk sample. Below these values, SPSS/PC+ prints a 95% confidence interval ("CI") for the difference between the observed and hypothesized means.

To the right of these values are the results of the *t*-test itself. The degrees of freedom (sample size minus one) and the two-tailed probability value ("2-tail Sig") are also computed. The result is considered statistically significant if the *p*-value is less than the chosen alpha level, usually .05 or .01. In this case, *p* is definitely less than .05 (and .01), so the result is considered statistically significant and the null hypothesis is rejected.

If you were doing the problem by hand, you would use a table in your statistics textbook to determine the critical *t*-value associated with 29 degrees of freedom—this value is 3.659 (for alpha = .05)—and then compare the observed *t*-value to the critical value. The observed *t*-value (3.90) is greater than the critical *t*-value, so you would reject the null hypothesis.

Note that the output from most statistical procedures in SPSS/PC+ works this same way. That is, SPSS/PC+ usually prints the *p*-value associated with the test statistic, and it is up to you to decide whether *p* is sufficiently small to reject the null hypothesis—that is, whether *p* is smaller than your chosen alpha. Both methods—comparing critical and observed *t*-values and comparing critical (alpha) and observed (*p*) probabilities—will lead to the same conclusion for any given problem.

•••••• 

# *Independent-Samples* t-*Test*

## *Sample Problem*

Professors in the psychology department at Rockhaven University conducted a study to determine the effectiveness of an integrated statistics/experimental methods course as opposed to the traditional method of offering the two courses separately. It was hypothesized that the students who took the integrated course would conduct better-quality (more controlled and statistically sound) research projects as a result of their more integrated training than would students in the traditional courses. To determine whether there is a difference in student performance, the final research projects of 20 students from an integrated course and 20 students from the traditional courses were evaluated. Their scores are listed in the table.

| *Student* | *Condition** | *Score* |
|---|---|---|
| 1 | 1 | 87 |
| 2 | 1 | 95 |
| 3 | 1 | 89 |
| 4 | 1 | 74 |
| 5 | 1 | 73 |
| 6 | 1 | 92 |
| 7 | 1 | 63 |
| 8 | 1 | 90 |
| 9 | 1 | 94 |
| 10 | 1 | 84 |
| 11 | 1 | 91 |
| 12 | 1 | 90 |
| 13 | 1 | 75 |
| 14 | 1 | 93 |
| 15 | 1 | 87 |
| 16 | 1 | 85 |
| 17 | 1 | 90 |
| 18 | 1 | 89 |
| 19 | 1 | 87 |
| 20 | 1 | 85 |
| 21 | 2 | 82 |
| 22 | 2 | 72 |
| 23 | 2 | 95 |
| 24 | 2 | 60 |
| 25 | 2 | 90 |

| *Student* | *Condition** | *Score* |
|---|---|---|
| 26 | 2 | 87 |
| 27 | 2 | 89 |
| 28 | 2 | 86 |
| 29 | 2 | 76 |
| 30 | 2 | 74 |
| 31 | 2 | 85 |
| 32 | 2 | 75 |
| 33 | 2 | 90 |
| 34 | 2 | 91 |
| 35 | 2 | 88 |
| 36 | 2 | 63 |
| 37 | 2 | 70 |
| 38 | 2 | 72 |
| 39 | 2 | 84 |
| 40 | 2 | 60 |

*For the conditions: 1 = integrated course, 2 = traditional courses.

In this problem, we are testing the null hypothesis that there is no difference in student performance as a result of the integrated course versus the traditional courses; that is, the mean difference between the conditions in the population from which the sample was drawn is zero. The alternative hypothesis reflects the expectation in the psychology department that the two types of courses differ in effectiveness.

## *Analysis*

```
DATA LIST FIXED / STUDENT 1-2 COND 4 SCORE 6-7.
BEGIN DATA.
 1 1 87
 2 1 95
 3 1 89
 4 1 74
 5 1 73
 6 1 92
 7 1 63
 8 1 90
 9 1 94
10 1 84
11 1 91
12 1 90
```

```
13 1 75
14 1 93
15 1 87
16 1 85
17 1 90
18 1 89
19 1 87
20 1 85
21 2 82
22 2 72
23 2 95
24 2 60
25 2 90
26 2 87
27 2 89
28 2 86
29 2 76
30 2 74
31 2 85
32 2 75
33 2 90
34 2 91
35 2 88
36 2 63
37 2 70
38 2 72
39 2 84
40 2 60
END DATA.
T-TEST /GROUPS COND (1,2) /VARIABLES SCORE.
```

The **T-TEST** command in SPSS/PC+ is used to test the null hypothesis that two population means are equal.

The subcommand **/GROUPS** is used to name the independent variable that you are using whose values identify the two groups you are comparing (in this problem, COND). After the independent variable name, you must type, in parentheses, the two values of this variable that identify the two groups you wish to compare (in this problem, 1 and 2). The two values must be separated with a comma.

The subcommand **/VARIABLES** is used to identify the dependent variable(s) (in this problem, SCORE) whose means you wish to compare between groups. You can specify several dependent variable names, separated by commas or spaces, if you wish.

*Important note:* Because the output from the **T-TEST** procedure looks very different in SPSS/PC+ Versions 4.0 and 5.0, both are displayed in this section.

*Annotated Output for Version 4:*

```
Independent samples of  COND

Group 1:  COND  EQ 1          Group 2:  COND  EQ 2

t-test for:  SCORE

                Number                   Standard    Standard
               of Cases       Mean      Deviation      Error

  Group 1         20        85.6500        8.242       1.843
  Group 2         20        79.4500       10.782       2.411


                 | Pooled Variance Estimate  | Separate Variance Estimate
                 |                           |
   F    2-Tail   |   t   Degrees of  2-Tail  |   t     Degrees of   2-Tail
 Value  Prob.    | Value   Freedom    Prob.  | Value     Freedom     Prob.
                 |                           |
  1.71   .250    |  2.04     38        .048  |  2.04      35.55       .049
```

When you execute the **T-TEST** command, SPSS/PC+ prints the means, standard deviations, and standard errors on the dependent variable separately for each group. In this case, the two groups are defined by the variable COND (1 = integrated, 2 = traditional).

Beneath the descriptive statistics are the results of statistical hypothesis tests. The "F Value" and associated "2-Tail Prob." refer to a test of the hypothesis that the two population variances are equal; this test probably is not of interest to you.

The information provided under "Separate Variance Estimate" reports the results of a *t*-test that is sometimes used when there is reason to believe that the two population variances are not equal. SPSS/PC+ reports the observed *t*-value, the degrees of freedom, and the two-tailed *p*-value. This test is often not discussed in introductory statistics courses, so if you haven't been introduced to this test, just ignore this part of the output.

The most commonly used test is the one listed under "Pooled Variance Estimate." Because we are assuming that the two population variances are equal, the pooled variance estimate combines the two sample variances to obtain the most accurate estimate of the variance common to both populations.

The observed $t$-value for this problem is 2.04, with degrees of freedom (total sample size minus two) equal to 38. The two-tailed probability of .048 is less than .05 and is therefore considered "significant," though barely, at the .05 level.

To verify this, you can use your statistics textbook to determine the critical $t$-value associated with 38 degrees of freedom: critical $t_{.05}(38)$ = approximately 2.03. The observed $t$-value (2.04) is greater (though barely) than the critical $t$-value; therefore, the null hypothesis is rejected at the .05 level of significance.

*Annotated Output for Version 5:*

```
t-tests for independent samples of  COND

                         Number
  Variable              of Cases    Mean          SD       SE of Mean
 -----------------------------------------------------------------------
  SCORE

  COND 1                    20     85.6500       8.242        1.843
  COND 2                    20     79.4500      10.782        2.411
 -----------------------------------------------------------------------

  Mean Difference = 6.2000

  Levene's Test for Equality of Variances: F= 3.880   P= .056

      t-test for Equality of Means                              95%
Variances  t-value   df    2-Tail Sig    SE of Diff      CI for Diff
-------------------------------------------------------------------------
Equal        2.04    38          .048        3.035      (.055, 12.345)
Unequal      2.04    35.55       .049        3.035      (.044, 12.356)
-------------------------------------------------------------------------
```

When you execute the **T-TEST** command, SPSS/PC+ prints the means, standard deviations, and standard errors on the dependent variable separately for each group. In this case, the two groups are defined by the variable COND (1 = integrated, 2 = traditional). Also included is the difference between the means of condition 1 and condition 2 (85.65 – 79.45 = 6.2).

Levene's test for equality of variances is also provided by SPSS/PC+. This test is probably not of interest to you at this point.

Beneath the descriptive statistics are the results of statistical hypothesis tests (*t*-tests for equality of means). The information provided in the row labeled "Unequal" reports the results of a *t*-test that is sometimes used when there is reason to believe that the two population variances are not equal. SPSS/PC+ reports the observed *t*-value, the degrees of freedom, and the two-tailed *p*-value ("2-Tail Sig"). This test is often not discussed in introductory statistics courses, so if you haven't been introduced to this test, just ignore this part of the output. Also reported on this line are the standard error of the difference scores ("SE of Diff") and the 95% confidence interval for the population mean of difference scores.

The most commonly used test is the one listed in the row labeled "Equal." Because we are assuming that the two population variances are equal, a pooled variance estimate is used to combine the two sample variances to obtain the most accurate estimate of the variance common to both populations.

The observed *t*-value for this problem is 2.04, with degrees of freedom (total sample size minus two) equal to 38. The two-tailed probability of .048 is less than .05 and is therefore considered "significant" (though barely) at the .05 level.

To verify this, you can use your statistics textbook to determine the critical *t*-value associated with 38 degrees of freedom: critical $t_{.05}(38)$ = approximately 2.03. The observed *t*-value (2.04) is greater, though barely, than the critical *t*-value; therefore, the null hypothesis is rejected at the .05 level of significance.

# *Dependent-Samples/Matched Pairs* t-*Test*

## *Sample Problem*

An investigator believes, based on past research, that parents who use positive verbal statements such as polite requests and suggestions have children who are more socially accepted and more positive in their interactions with peers. Although children acquire behavioral information from sources other than parents (for example, TV and peers), more induction—coaching children by introducing consequences for behaviors and supplying rationales that support them—on the part of parents, as opposed to more power-assertive and permissive types of discipline, facilitates a prosocial behavioral orientation in children that leads to greater social competency and greater acceptance by peers. Twenty first-grade children, who were rated by teachers and peers as aggressive, and their parents were selected for a study to determine whether a seminar with instruction on inductive parenting techniques improves social competency in children. The parents attended the seminar for one month. The children were tested for social competency before the course began, and they were retested six months after the completion of the course. The results of the social competency test are shown in the table (with higher scores indicating greater social competency).

| *Child* | *Pre-Seminar* | *Post-Seminar* |
|---|---|---|
| 1 | 31 | 34 |
| 2 | 26 | 25 |
| 3 | 32 | 38 |
| 4 | 38 | 36 |
| 5 | 29 | 29 |
| 6 | 34 | 41 |
| 7 | 24 | 26 |
| 8 | 35 | 42 |
| 9 | 30 | 36 |
| 10 | 36 | 44 |
| 11 | 31 | 28 |
| 12 | 27 | 32 |
| 13 | 25 | 25 |
| 14 | 28 | 30 |
| 15 | 32 | 41 |
| 16 | 27 | 37 |
| 17 | 37 | 39 |
| 18 | 29 | 33 |
| 19 | 31 | 40 |
| 20 | 27 | 28 |

In this problem, we are testing the null hypothesis that there is no difference between the means of pre- and post-seminar social competency scores. In other words, the parenting seminar has no effect on children's social competency scores or, stated yet another way, the population mean of difference scores (pre-seminar minus post-seminar scores) equals zero. The alternative hypothesis reflects the investigator's belief that there is a difference between pairs of pre- and post-seminar scores; the population mean of difference scores does not equal zero.

## *Analysis*

```
DATA LIST FIXED / CHILD 1-2 PRE 4-5 POST 7-8.
BEGIN DATA.
 1 31 34
 2 26 25
 3 32 38
 4 38 36
 5 29 29
 6 34 41
 7 24 26
 8 35 42
 9 30 36
10 36 44
11 31 28
12 27 32
13 25 25
14 28 30
15 32 41
16 27 37
17 37 39
18 29 33
19 31 40
20 27 28
END DATA.
T-TEST /PAIRS PRE POST.
```

Again, the **T-TEST** command in SPSS/PC+ is used to test the null hypothesis that two population means are equal.

The **/PAIRS** subcommand tells SPSS/PC+ that you wish to conduct a paired *t*-test to determine whether the means of two variables are equal. After the

**/PAIRS** subcommand, you must specify the names of the two variables whose means you wish to compare. In this example these variables are **PRE** and **POST**.

*Important note:* Because the output from the **T-TEST** procedure looks very different in SPSS/PC+ Versions 4.0 and 5.0, both are displayed in this section.

*Annotated Output for Version 4:*

```
. . . . . . . . . . . . . . . . . . . . . . . . . . . . . . . . . . . . . . .

Paired samples t-test:   PRE
                         POST

Variable      Number                   Standard   Standard
             of Cases       Mean      Deviation     Error

PRE             20        30.4500       4.019        .899
POST            20        34.2000       6.066       1.356


(Difference) Standard    Standard |        2-Tail |   t    Degrees of   2-Tail
     Mean    Deviation      Error | Corr.  Prob.  | Value    Freedom     Prob.
                                  |               |
   -3.7500      3.919        .876 |  .771   .000  | -4.28       19        .000
. . . . . . . . . . . . . . . . . . . . . . . . . . . . . . . . . . . . . . .
```

When you execute the **T-TEST** command, SPSS/PC+ produces some descriptive statistics (number of cases, mean, standard deviation, and standard error) for each variable (in this case, PRE and POST).

A paired *t*-test is calculated by first computing a set of difference scores in which one variable is subtracted from the other (in this case, PRE minus POST). The mean of these difference scores is given under "(Difference) Mean" and is equivalent to the difference between the mean of PRE and the mean of POST. The standard deviation and standard error of these difference scores are listed next.

At the far right of the output are the results of the *t*-test itself, which is computed as

$$t = \frac{\text{Difference mean}}{\text{Estimated standard error}} = \frac{-3.75}{0.876} = -4.28$$

The degrees of freedom (number of pairs of observations minus one) and the two-tailed probability value (*p*-value) are also printed. Note that although the computed *p*-value for this problem is reported as ".000," this does not mean that the *p*-value is actually equal to zero. SPSS/PC+ rounds off *p*-values (in this case, to three decimal places). Therefore, any *p*-value less than .0005 is printed as .000.

To check this, you can use your statistics textbook to determine the critical *t*-value associated with 19 degrees of freedom and a *p*-value of .001 (since this is the smallest level of significance listed in most textbooks) for a two-tailed test: critical $t_{.001}(19) = 3.883$. The observed *t*-value is greater than the critical *t*-value; therefore, the null hypothesis is rejected at the .001 level of significance.

Incidentally, SPSS/PC+ also calculates the correlation coefficient for the two variables PRE and POST and the two-tailed probability for a test of the null hypothesis that the population correlation coefficient equals zero. These results appear under "Corr." and "2-Tail Prob." in the middle of the output. This test is probably not of interest to you at this point. A more direct way of calculating correlation coefficients is presented in a later section of this manual.

*Annotated Output for Version 5:*

```
- - - t-tests for paired samples - - -

             Number of           2-tail
Variable       pairs      Corr    Sig         Mean        SD      SE of Mean
------------------------------------------------------------------------------
PRE                                          30.4500     4.019         .899
                20        .771   .000
POST                                         34.2000     6.066        1.356
------------------------------------------------------------------------------

          Paired Differences          |
Mean            SD         SE of Mean |      t-value      df   2-tail Sig
------------------------------------------------------------------------------
-3.7500        3.919          .876    |      -4.28        19        .000
95% CI (-5.584, -1.916)               |
```

When you execute the **T-TEST** command, SPSS/PC+ produces some descriptive statistics (number of cases, mean, standard deviation, and standard error) for each variable (in this case, PRE and POST).

A paired *t*-test is calculated by first computing a set of difference scores in which one variable is subtracted from the other (in this case, PRE minus POST). The mean of these difference scores is given under "Paired Differences" and is equivalent to the difference between the mean of PRE and the mean of POST. The standard deviation ("SD") and standard error ("SE of Mean") of these difference scores are listed next. Below these values is printed a 95% confidence interval ("CI") for the mean of the difference scores.

At the far right of the output are the results of the *t*-test itself, which is computed as

$$t = \frac{\text{Difference mean}}{\text{Estimated standard error}} = \frac{-3.75}{0.876} = -4.28$$

The degrees of freedom (number of pairs of observations minus one) and the two-tailed probability value (*p*-value) are also printed. Note that although the computed *p*-value for this problem is reported as ".000," this does not mean that the *p*-value is actually equal to zero. SPSS/PC+ rounds off *p*-values—in this case, to three decimal places. Therefore, any *p*-value less than .0005 is printed as .000.

To check this, you can use your statistics textbook to determine the critical t-value associated with 19 degrees of freedom and a *p*-value of .001 (since this is the smallest level of significance listed in most textbooks) for a two-tailed test: critical $t_{.001}(19) = 3.883$. The observed *t*-value is greater than the critical *t*-value; therefore, the null hypothesis is rejected at the .001 level of significance.

Incidentally, SPSS/PC+ also calculates the correlation coefficient for the two variables PRE and POST and the two-tailed probability for a test of the null hypothesis that the population correlation coefficient equals zero. These results appear under "Corr" and "2-tail Sig" in the middle of the output. This test is probably not of interest to you at this point. A more direct way of calculating correlation coefficients is presented in a later section.

# One-Way Between-Groups ANOVA

## Sample Problem

Sleep researchers have postulated that, in a broad evolutionary sense, sleeping more poorly during periods of perceived environmental threat may have survival value. Previous research has indicated that individuals who are experiencing anxiety or stress exhibit reduced periods of deep sleep and increased periods of light sleep. (One can most easily be aroused by a sound in the environment while in light sleep.) An attachment researcher conducted a study to examine the effects of anxious, avoidant, and secure attachment styles on the physiology of sleep. The investigator hypothesized that children with anxious (and perhaps avoidant) attachment styles experience more sleep disturbances than children with secure attachment styles because they feel responsible for monitoring the external environment and regulating the distance between themselves and their caregivers. These children may find it difficult to sleep when their caregivers are physically absent, and they may develop patterns of light sleep because of the need to be aware of the caregiver's presence at all times. Deep sleep can be experienced as threatening to the attachment bond and thus dangerous to the child. The sleep patterns of ten secure, ten anxious, and ten avoidant 5-year-old children were monitored. Of primary importance to the attachment researcher was the overall percentage of time that each child spent in deep (delta) sleep. It was hypothesized that children who are insecurely attached to their primary caregivers will spend a lower percentage of time in deep (delta) sleep as compared to their secure counterparts. The table lists the average amount of time that each child spent in delta sleep, expressed as a percentage of total sleep time.

| *Subject* | *Attachment Style** | *Delta Sleep* |
|---|---|---|
| 1 | 1 | 21 |
| 2 | 1 | 21 |
| 3 | 1 | 25 |
| 4 | 1 | 23 |
| 5 | 1 | 24 |
| 6 | 1 | 23 |
| 7 | 1 | 23 |
| 8 | 1 | 22 |
| 9 | 1 | 22 |
| 10 | 1 | 22 |
| 11 | 2 | 17 |

| *Subject* | *Attachment Style** | *Delta Sleep* |
|---|---|---|
| 12 | 2 | 17 |
| 13 | 2 | 15 |
| 14 | 2 | 15 |
| 15 | 2 | 15 |
| 16 | 2 | 14 |
| 17 | 2 | 20 |
| 18 | 2 | 13 |
| 19 | 2 | 14 |
| 20 | 2 | 19 |
| 21 | 3 | 18 |
| 22 | 3 | 20 |
| 23 | 3 | 18 |
| 24 | 3 | 19 |
| 25 | 3 | 17 |
| 26 | 3 | 17 |
| 27 | 3 | 15 |
| 28 | 3 | 16 |
| 29 | 3 | 17 |
| 30 | 3 | 18 |

*For the attachment styles: 1 = secure, 2 = anxious, 3 = avoidant.

In this problem, we are testing the null hypothesis that, on average, the three populations of children (with secure, anxious, and avoidant attachment styles) spend equal percentages of time in deep (delta) sleep:

$$H_O = \begin{matrix}\text{Mean delta for} \\ \text{population of} \\ \text{secure children}\end{matrix} = \begin{matrix}\text{Mean delta for} \\ \text{population of} \\ \text{anxious children}\end{matrix} = \begin{matrix}\text{Mean delta for} \\ \text{population of} \\ \text{avoidant children}\end{matrix}$$

## *Analysis: One-Way Between-Groups ANOVA*

```
DATA LIST FIXED / SUBJECT 1-2 ATTSTYLE 4 DELTA 6-7.
BEGIN DATA.
 1 1 21
 2 1 21
 3 1 25
 4 1 23
 5 1 24
 6 1 23
 7 1 23
 8 1 22
 9 1 22
```

```
10 1 22
11 2 17
12 2 17
13 2 15
14 2 15
15 2 15
16 2 14
17 2 20
18 2 13
19 2 14
20 2 19
21 3 18
22 3 20
23 3 18
24 3 19
25 3 17
26 3 17
27 3 15
28 3 16
29 3 17
30 3 18
END DATA.
ONEWAY /VARIABLES DELTA BY ATTSTYLE (1,3) /STATISTICS 1.
```

The **ONEWAY** command in SPSS/PC+ is one of several ways to conduct a one-way analysis of variance. We use **ONEWAY** here because it has several useful subcommands for conducting "multiple comparison" tests, as illustrated in subsequent sections.

The subcommand **/VARIABLES** is required to specify the variables to be used in the analysis. After the **/VARIABLES** subcommand, you must type the name(s) of the dependent variable(s) whose means you wish to test for each level of the independent variable. In this problem, the dependent variable is DELTA. After typing the name of the dependent variable, you must type the word BY, and then type the name of your independent variable. In this problem, the independent variable is ATTSTYLE. After typing the name of your independent variable, you must type, in parentheses and separated by a comma, the values of the lowest- and highest-numbered groups to be included in the analysis. In this case, we want to include ATTSTYLE groups 1, 2, and 3; so we type **(1,3)**.

The **/STATISTICS 1** subcommand tells SPSS/PC+ to provide group descriptive statistics, including the count, mean, standard deviation, standard error, 95% confidence limits for the mean, and the minimum and maximum values for each group.

```
- - - - - - - - - - - O N E W A Y - - - - - - - - - - -

     Variable  DELTA
  By Variable  ATTSTYLE

                              Analysis of Variance

                                Sum of         Mean            F      F
       Source          D.F.    Squares       Squares         Ratio  Prob.

Between Groups            2     244.8667      122.4333       41.4248  .0000

Within Groups            27      79.8000        2.9556

Total                    29     324.6667
```

```
- - - - - - - - - - - O N E W A Y - - - - - - - - - - -

                                 Standard   Standard
Group      Count        Mean    Deviation     Error     95 Pct Conf Int for Mean

Grp 1         10     22.6000       1.2649     .4000     21.6951  To     23.5049
Grp 2         10     15.9000       2.2828     .7219     14.2670  To     17.5330
Grp 3         10     17.5000       1.4337     .4534     16.4744  To     18.5256

Total         30     18.6667       3.3460     .6109     17.4173  To     19.9161


Group         Minimum     Maximum

Grp 1         21.0000     25.0000
Grp 2         13.0000     20.0000
Grp 3         15.0000     20.0000

Total         13.0000     25.0000
```

When you execute the **ONEWAY** command, SPSS/PC+ produces a standard ANOVA table for the one-way analysis of variance.

Three sources of variability are listed: "Between Groups" (variability due to the treatment effect—differences between groups as a result of attachment style), "Within Groups" (variability reflecting random error), and "Total." For each, SPSS/PC+ reports the degrees of freedom, sum of squares, and mean square (sum of squares divided by degrees of freedom).

The "F Ratio," calculated as the mean square between divided by the mean square within, is listed next in the output. The $F$ ratio in this example equals 41.4248, and its associated $p$-value ("F Prob.") is reported as .0000. (As in previous examples, this does not mean that $p$ is exactly equal to zero, but rather that the probability is less than .00005 and has been rounded off to .0000.) Thus, we reject the null hypothesis and conclude that the three attachment styles differ with respect to the mean amounts of time that children spend in deep (delta) sleep.

## *Analysis: Post Hoc Tests for One-Way Between-Groups ANOVA*

Rejection of the overall ("omnibus") null hypothesis in ANOVA tells us only that not all population means are equal. It does not indicate which attachment groups are significantly different from which other ones. One way to further examine group differences is to use "post hoc" or "a posteriori" multiple comparison tests.

```
ONEWAY /VARIABLES DELTA BY ATTSTYLE (1,3) /RANGES TUKEY.
```

To request a test of multiple comparisons, simply add the **/RANGES** subcommand to the end of your **ONEWAY** command line. This subcommand tells SPSS/PC+ to conduct multiple comparison tests for all possible differences among the group means.

After the **/RANGES** subcommand, you must select a multiple comparison test. In this example, we have selected the **TUKEY** "honestly significant difference" test. Other options include **/RANGES DUNCAN** (for Duncan multiple range tests), **/RANGES SNK** (for Student-Newman-Keuls tests), and **/RANGES SCHEFFE** (for Scheffe's test).

```
. . . . . . . . . . . . . . . . . . . . . . . . . . . . . . . . . . . . . . . . . . . . . .

              - - - - - - - - - - - O N E W A Y - - - - - - - - - - -

     Variable  DELTA
   By Variable  ATTSTYLE


Multiple Range Test


Tukey-HSD Procedure
Ranges for the  .050 level -

         3.50   3.50

The ranges above are table ranges.
The value actually compared with Mean(J)-Mean(I) is..
       1.2156 * Range * Sqrt(1/N(I) + 1/N(J))


(*) Denotes pairs of groups significantly different at the  .050 level
. . . . . . . . . . . . . . . . . . . . . . . . . . . . . . . . . . . . . . . . . . . . . .
. . . . . . . . . . . . . . . . . . . . . . . . . . . . . . . . . . . . . . . . . . . . . .

              - - - - - - - - - - - O N E W A Y - - - - - - - - - - -

     Variable  DELTA
     (Continued)


                           G G G
                           r r r
                           p p p

    Mean       Group       2 3 1

   15.9000     Grp 2
   17.5000     Grp 3
   22.6000     Grp 1       * *
. . . . . . . . . . . . . . . . . . . . . . . . . . . . . . . . . . . . . . . . . . . . . .
```

```
 Homogeneous Subsets (Subsets of groups, whose highest and lowest means
                      do not differ by more than the shortest
                      significant range for a subset of that size)

SUBSET  1

Group        Grp 2        Grp 3
Mean       15.9000      17.5000
- - - - - - - - - - - - - - - - -

SUBSET  2

Group        Grp 1
Mean       22.6000
- - - - - - - - - -
```

When you execute this command, SPSS/PC+ first produces an ANOVA table exactly like the output in the previous example. (Because it is identical to the ANOVA table already shown, this section of the output has been deleted here.) SPSS/PC+ then produces a matrix of all attachment groups by all attachment groups. Asterisks are used to indicate which groups differ significantly on the dependent variable DELTA. (*Note:* The default significance level for all tests on the **/RANGES** subcommand is .05.)

The last part of the output describes these results in a different way. Groups that do not differ significantly from each other are placed into homogeneous subsets. In this example, groups 2 and 3 form a homogeneous subset (they don't differ from each other), but group 1 forms a separate subset because both groups 2 and 3 differ significantly from group 1. Sometimes these results are written as follows:

```
Group 1      Group 2      Group 3
_______      ______________________
```

where the underlines are used to indicate homogeneous subsets.

## *Analysis: Planned Comparisons for One-Way Between-Groups ANOVA*

Another approach to multiple comparisons in ANOVA is to test more specific hypotheses, which have been specified in advance, about which means differ from which other means or which combinations of means differ from other combinations of means. These tests are known as "planned comparisons," "contrasts," or "a priori" multiple comparison tests.

```
ONEWAY /VARIABLES DELTA BY ATTSTYLE (1,3)
       /CONTRAST -2 1 1
       /CONTRAST 0 1 -1.
```

The **ONEWAY /VARIABLES DELTA BY ATTSTYLE (1,3)** command line is identical to that used in the previous example. However, contrasts allow you to make planned comparisons of two specific groups, or two combinations of groups, and they provide an alternative to the post hoc multiple comparisons tests offered with the **/RANGES** subcommand, as described previously.

In this problem, we are testing two contrasts. (Incidentally, these particular contrasts happen to be "orthogonal" contrasts.) For each contrast, we are testing a different null hypothesis. Both contrasts are described here.

*Contrast 1.* First, we want to test the null hypothesis that the mean percentage of time spent in delta sleep for the population of secure children is equal to the mean of the mean times for the populations of anxious and avoidant children:

$$H_O: \begin{matrix}\text{Mean delta for}\\ \text{population of}\\ \text{secure children}\end{matrix} = \frac{\begin{matrix}\text{Mean delta for}\\ \text{population of}\\ \text{anxious children}\end{matrix} + \begin{matrix}\text{Mean delta for}\\ \text{population of}\\ \text{avoidant children}\end{matrix}}{2}$$

*Contrast 2.* Next, we want to test the null hypothesis that the mean percentage of time spent in delta sleep for the population of anxious children is equal to the mean percentage of time spent in delta sleep for the population of avoidant children:

$$H_O: \begin{matrix}\text{Mean delta for}\\ \text{population of}\\ \text{anxious children}\end{matrix} = \begin{matrix}\text{Mean delta for}\\ \text{population of}\\ \text{avoidant children}\end{matrix}$$

Therefore, our contrast coefficients for this problem, for groups 1, 2, and 3 in order, are as follows:

| | | | |
|---|---|---|---|
| Contrast 1: | –2 | 1 | 1 |
| Contrast 2: | 0 | 1 | –1 |

You can tell SPSS/PC+ which groups to compare by using the subcommand **/CONTRAST**. After each **/CONTRAST** subcommand, simply type the numerical codes for the groups you wish to contrast in order from the lowest- to highest-numbered groups. You can type as many **CONTRAST** subcommands as you wish in a given **ONEWAY** command.

```
- - - - - - - - - - - O N E W A Y - - - - - - - - - -

     Variable  DELTA
  By Variable  ATTSTYLE


 Contrast Coefficient Matrix

           Grp 1        Grp 3
                 Grp 2

Contrast  1  -2.0   1.0   1.0

Contrast  2    .0   1.0  -1.0
```

```
- - - - - - - - - - - O N E W A Y - - - - - - - - - -

                                    Pooled Variance Estimate
                  Value       S. Error        T Value    D.F.      T Prob.

Contrast  1     -11.8000        1.3317         -8.861    27.0         .000

Contrast  2      -1.6000         .7688         -2.081    27.0         .047


                                  Separate Variance Estimate
                  Value       S. Error        T Value    D.F.      T Prob.

Contrast  1     -11.8000        1.1690        -10.094    23.2         .000

Contrast  2      -1.6000         .8524         -1.877    15.1         .080
```

When you execute the **ONEWAY** command using contrasts, SPSS/PC+ first produces the traditional ANOVA table for the overall ("omnibus") null hypothesis that all three population means are equal. (This has been deleted here to save space.)

Next, SPSS/PC+ produces a contrast coefficient matrix—just a reminder about which groups were assigned which coefficients for each test—followed by the significance tests for each contrast. SPSS/PC+ provides significance tests for both pooled and separate variance estimates. The more commonly used test is the one listed under "Pooled Variance Estimate."

For each contrast, SPSS/PC+ prints: (1) the value of the contrast itself, a linear combination of the contrast coefficients and sample means (labeled "Value" in the output); (2) a standard error ("S. Error"); (3) the observed *t*-statistic ("T Value"); (4) the error degrees of freedom ("D.F.") for the test; and (5) a two-tailed probability or *p*-value ("T. Prob.").

You might learn in class that contrasts are calculated by using *F* tests rather than *t*-tests. In fact, either can be used and they produce identical results. SPSS/PC+ just happens to present the *t* results rather than the *F* results. For each contrast, you may just square the observed *t*-value produced by SPSS/PC+ to find the corresponding *F* value.

## Two-Way Between-Groups ANOVA

### Sample Problem

A male psychology student has been interested in dating one of his female colleagues all year; however, he is uncertain about how to approach her and introduce himself. He knows that first impressions are very important, and he feels that the way he presents himself initially will determine the course of their relationship. Since he is a psychology student and is familiar with research methodology, he decides to conduct a study to determine the effectiveness of various approaches to meeting someone. The three approaches he wants to investigate are: (1) casual conversation approach (engaging in casual conversation with the woman, saying whatever comes naturally), (2) humor approach (the initial use of humor to break the ice and to generate interest in the woman), and (3) pick-up line approach (the use of a clever pick-up line to express interest and to generate interest in the woman). The researcher also feels that his attractiveness may have an impact on the effectiveness of each approach; therefore, he decides to include attractiveness as a second independent variable. To help him conduct the study, he recruits two male friends who have a pleasant, friendly personality similar to his own. One of his friends has been consistently rated by a random sample of women as attractive, and the other has been consistently rated as unattractive. The study is conducted with a random selection of 30 female students who are sitting alone in the student union lounge. The attractive confederate accosts five women using the "casual conversation approach," five women using the "humor approach," and five women using the "pick-up line approach." The unattractive confederate also accosts different sets of five women with each approach. The measure of success for each approach is the length of time (in minutes) that the confederates are able to engage each woman in conversation. The results are listed in the table.

| *Subject* | *Attractiveness** | *Approach*† | *Time* |
|---|---|---|---|
| 1 | 1 | 1 | 43 |
| 2 | 1 | 1 | 35 |
| 3 | 1 | 1 | 52 |
| 4 | 1 | 1 | 48 |
| 5 | 1 | 1 | 30 |
| 6 | 1 | 2 | 61 |
| 7 | 1 | 2 | 45 |
| 8 | 1 | 2 | 52 |
| 9 | 1 | 2 | 39 |

| *Subject* | *Attractiveness** | *Approach†* | *Time* |
|---|---|---|---|
| 10 | 1 | 2 | 43 |
| 11 | 1 | 3 | 1 |
| 12 | 1 | 3 | 2 |
| 13 | 1 | 3 | 3 |
| 14 | 1 | 3 | 2 |
| 15 | 1 | 3 | 4 |
| 16 | 2 | 1 | 15 |
| 17 | 2 | 1 | 22 |
| 18 | 2 | 1 | 10 |
| 19 | 2 | 1 | 27 |
| 20 | 2 | 1 | 20 |
| 21 | 2 | 2 | 60 |
| 22 | 2 | 2 | 42 |
| 23 | 2 | 2 | 53 |
| 24 | 2 | 2 | 40 |
| 25 | 2 | 2 | 39 |
| 26 | 2 | 3 | 2 |
| 27 | 2 | 3 | 3 |
| 28 | 2 | 3 | 1 |
| 29 | 2 | 3 | 1 |
| 30 | 2 | 3 | 4 |

*For attractiveness: 1 = attractive, 2 = unattractive.
†For approach: 1 = conversation, 2 = humor, 3 = pick-up line.

A two-way ANOVA will test three null hypotheses corresponding to (1) the main effect of attractiveness, (2) the main effect of approach type, and (3) the interaction of attractiveness and approach type.

## *Analysis*

```
DATA LIST FIXED / SUBJECT 1-2 ATTRACT 4 APPROACH 6 TIME 8-9.
BEGIN DATA.
 1 1 1 43
 2 1 1 35
 3 1 1 52
 4 1 1 48
 5 1 1 30
 6 1 2 61
 7 1 2 45
 8 1 2 52
 9 1 2 39
10 1 2 43
```

```
11 1 3  1
12 1 3  2
13 1 3  3
14 1 3  2
15 1 3  4
16 2 1 15
17 2 1 22
18 2 1 10
19 2 1 27
20 2 1 20
21 2 2 60
22 2 2 42
23 2 2 53
24 2 2 40
25 2 2 39
26 2 3  2
27 2 3  3
28 2 3  1
29 2 3  1
30 2 3  4
END DATA.
MANOVA TIME BY ATTRACT (1,2) APPROACH (1,3) /OMEANS /DESIGN.
```

The **MANOVA** (multivariate analysis of variance) command in SPSS/PC+ can be used to analyze univariate as well as multivariate designs (those with several dependent variables). Here, we are using the **MANOVA** command to conduct a two-way analysis of variance.

After the **MANOVA** command, you must type the name of your dependent variable. In this example, the dependent variable is TIME. Then you must type the word BY, followed by the names of your between-subjects factors (i.e., independent variables). In this example, our independent variables are ATTRACT and APPROACH. After typing the name of each independent variable, you must type, in parentheses, the value of its lowest code, a comma, and then the value of its highest code. In this example, the independent variable ATTRACT is followed by **(1,2)**, which identifies the minimum and maximum values for the two levels of this factor (1 = attractive, 2 = unattractive). The independent variable name APPROACH is followed by **(1,3)**, which identifies the minimum and maximum values for the three levels of this factor (1 = conversation, 2 = humor, 3 = pick-up line).

The **/OMEANS** (observed means) subcommand tells SPSS/PC+ to produce the observed means of the dependent variable for the levels of each factor (independent variable).

The **/DESIGN** subcommand simply tells SPSS/PC+ to run the analysis according to the requested specifications. It tells SPSS/PC+ to produce the significance tests along with other requested output (observed means). SPSS/PC+ will produce a full factorial model that contains all the factors named in the **MANOVA** command and the interactions among the factors. The **/DESIGN** subcommand must always be the last specification in the **MANOVA** command.

```
 30 cases accepted.
  0 cases rejected because of out-of-range factor values.
  0 cases rejected because of missing data.
  6 non-empty cells.

  1 design will be processed.

- - - - - - - - - -
Cell Means and Standard Deviations
Variable .. TIME
     FACTOR          CODE                 Mean  Std. Dev.            N

 ATTRACT              1
  APPROACH             1                41.600     9.072             5
  APPROACH             2                48.000     8.660             5
  APPROACH             3                 2.400     1.140             5
 ATTRACT              2
  APPROACH             1                18.800     6.535             5
  APPROACH             2                46.800     9.257             5
  APPROACH             3                 2.200     1.304             5
For entire sample                       26.633    21.025            30
```

```
* * ANALYSIS  OF  VARIANCE — DESIGN   1 * *

Cell Means and Standard Deviations  (CONT.)
Tests of Significance for TIME using UNIQUE sums of squares
Source of Variation           SS      DF        MS          F  Sig of F

WITHIN CELLS             1154.80      24     48.12
CONSTANT                21280.03       1  21280.03     442.26      .000
ATTRACT                   488.03       1    488.03      10.14      .004
APPROACH                10360.87       2   5180.43     107.66      .000
ATTRACT BY APPROACH       815.27       2    407.63       8.47      .002

- - - - - - - - - -
```

When you execute the **MANOVA** command, the **/OMEANS** output appears first. The cell means and standard deviations of the dependent variable **TIME** are given for each level of each independent variable.

These means might be arranged, in accordance with the "two-way" nature of the design, as follows:

| *ATTRACT* | | *APPROACH* | | | |
|---|---|---|---|---|---|
| | | *1 = Conversation* | *2 = Humor* | *3 = Pick-Up Line* | |
| | *1 = Attractive* | 41.60 | 48.00 | 2.40 | 30.67 |
| | *2 = Unattractive* | 18.80 | 46.80 | 2.20 | 22.60 |
| | | 30.20 | 47.40 | 2.30 | |

The means within the six cells were taken directly from the printout. However, note that the "marginal means"—the overall means for each row and column written at the margins of the table—did not appear in the printout. You will need to calculate these yourself, as we have in this example, as the mean of the cell means across each respective column and row.

Next, SPSS/PC+ produces an ANOVA table for the two-way analysis of variance. In this example, the three sources of between-groups variability are listed: (1) ATTRACT (variability between rows in the table, representing the average effect of attractiveness), (2) APPROACH (variability between columns in the table, representing the average effect of approach type), and (3) ATTRACT BY APPROACH (variability between groups resulting from the unique joint effect of the two factors in combination, representing the interaction of the two independent variables).

CONSTANT is an additional source of "variability" that automatically is listed and tested by SPSS/PC+. You can safely disregard this line of the output, since it is of no interest to us in most cases. In case you're curious, this line presents a test of the null hypothesis that all of the measures have means of zero in the population. In the present example, it should be obvious that this is really a meaningless hypothesis; in fact, we know it is false. What we want to know instead is whether the means differ from each other across conditions, and the test of CONSTANT is entirely irrelevant for our purposes.

Because three different null hypotheses are being tested, three different significance tests are conducted. Three different *F* ratios are produced, along with their associated *p*-values ("Sig of F"). The information necessary to obtain the *F* ratios is also printed: sums of squares ("SS"), degrees of freedom ("DF"), and mean squares ("MS").

In this problem, these are the three *F* ratios:

$$F_{\text{attract}} = \frac{488.03}{48.12} = 10.14; \quad F_{\text{approach}} = \frac{5180.43}{48.12} = 107.66; \quad F_{\text{inter}} = \frac{407.63}{48.12} = 8.47$$

The *p*-values for these *F* ratios are listed under "Sig of F": They equal .004, .000 (that is, less than .0005), and .002, respectively. In this case, all three *p*-values are sufficiently small to reject the respective null hypotheses at the .05 or .01 level. Both main effects and the interaction are statistically significant.

• • • • • •

# One-Way Within-Subjects ANOVA

## Sample Problem

The facilitator of a stress management therapy group conducted a study to determine the most effective relaxation technique(s) for reducing stress. The 20 members of his stress management group participated in the study. The heart rate of each participant was monitored during each of five conditions. Each participant experienced all five conditions during the same session to control for variations in the amount of stress experienced from day to day. The five conditions were as follows: (1) baseline (subjects sat quietly for 15 minutes); (2) guided meditation (subjects listened to a tape instructing them to close their eyes, breathe deeply, and relax their muscles for 15 minutes while concentrating on a single word or phrase); (3) comedy (subjects listened to the act of a stand-up comedian on a tape cassette for 15 minutes); (4) nature (subjects listened to a tape for 15 minutes of various sounds of nature, including the sounds of the ocean, wind, rain, leaves rustling, and birds chirping); and (5) music (subjects listened to a tape of easy-listening music for 15 minutes). Every subject experienced the baseline condition first; however, the four treatment conditions were counterbalanced to eliminate the possibility of order effects. Each subject's heart rate was monitored continuously during each of the 15-minute intervals. The mean heart rates (beats per minute) for each subject during each condition are listed in the table.

| *Subject* | *Baseline* | *Meditation* | *Comedy* | *Nature* | *Music* |
|---|---|---|---|---|---|
| 1 | 85 | 70 | 75 | 71 | 74 |
| 2 | 79 | 69 | 73 | 70 | 72 |
| 3 | 91 | 82 | 87 | 83 | 86 |
| 4 | 93 | 80 | 85 | 79 | 84 |
| 5 | 92 | 80 | 86 | 81 | 87 |
| 6 | 87 | 79 | 83 | 80 | 81 |
| 7 | 84 | 72 | 77 | 73 | 76 |
| 8 | 78 | 69 | 74 | 71 | 73 |
| 9 | 79 | 69 | 73 | 70 | 72 |
| 10 | 80 | 71 | 74 | 72 | 73 |
| 11 | 80 | 72 | 76 | 74 | 75 |
| 12 | 97 | 80 | 89 | 82 | 87 |
| 13 | 88 | 78 | 82 | 80 | 82 |
| 14 | 94 | 79 | 84 | 80 | 84 |
| 15 | 75 | 60 | 68 | 62 | 66 |
| 16 | 76 | 67 | 72 | 69 | 70 |
| 17 | 90 | 77 | 83 | 76 | 83 |

| *Subject* | *Baseline* | *Meditation* | *Comedy* | *Nature* | *Music* |
|---|---|---|---|---|---|
| 18 | 86 | 75 | 80 | 77 | 80 |
| 19 | 94 | 84 | 88 | 85 | 87 |
| 20 | 70 | 59 | 64 | 58 | 62 |

In this problem, we are testing the null hypothesis that, on the average, the heart rates of subjects remain the same during each of the five conditions (the baseline condition and the four relaxation conditions). That is, the population means for all five conditions are equal or, alternatively, these conditions do not influence heart rate.

## *Analysis*

```
DATA LIST FIXED / SUBJECT 1-2 BASELINE 4-5 MEDITATE 7-8 COMEDY 10-11
                  NATURE 13-14 MUSIC 16-17.
BEGIN DATA.
 1 85 70 75 71 74
 2 79 69 73 70 72
 3 91 82 87 83 86
 4 93 80 85 79 84
 5 92 80 86 81 87
 6 87 79 83 80 81
 7 84 72 77 73 76
 8 78 69 74 71 73
 9 79 69 73 70 72
10 80 71 74 72 73
11 80 72 76 74 75
12 97 80 89 82 87
13 88 78 82 80 82
14 94 79 84 80 84
15 75 60 68 62 66
16 76 67 72 69 70
17 90 77 83 76 83
18 86 75 80 77 80
19 94 84 88 85 87
20 70 59 64 58 62
END DATA.
MANOVA BASELINE MEDITATE COMEDY NATURE MUSIC
       /WSFACTORS COND (5)
       /PRINT SIGNIF (AVONLY)
       /OMEANS
       /DESIGN.
```

The **MANOVA** command in SPSS/PC+ can be used to analyze a variety of univariate and multivariate designs, including those in which the same variable is measured more than once for each subject. Here, we are using the **MANOVA** command to conduct a one-way within-subjects (repeated measures) analysis of variance.

When conducting a repeated measures analysis using **MANOVA**, you must set up your data so that the repeated measurements are different variables. Notice that, although we are measuring the same thing (heart rate) for each subject under all five conditions, the data values are entered as if there were five separate variables. Each of these variables represents a different level of the within-subjects factor (heart rate).

After the **MANOVA** command, you must type the names of the dependent variables that represent the various conditions or levels of the independent variable. In this example, our variable names are BASELINE, MEDITATE, COMEDY, NATURE, and MUSIC. Each dependent variable listed represents heart rate measured at different times for the same subject.

The subcommand **/WSFACTORS** (within subjects factors) must be the first subcommand typed after the variable names. Then you must type a name for your within-subjects factor. This *cannot* be the name of one of your existing variables. In this example, we chose the name **COND** (for "condition") for the independent variable. Next, you must type, in parentheses, the number of levels for the within-subjects factor. In this example, heart rate is measured under five different conditions; therefore, there are **(5)** levels of our within-subjects factor COND. This tells SPSS/PC+ that we do not really have five separate dependent variables, but rather five levels of one independent variable called COND.

The subcommand **/PRINT** controls the output printed by SPSS/PC+. The word **SIGNIF** following the **/PRINT** subcommand allows you to request, or suppress, significance tests. **(AVONLY)** tells SPSS/PC+ to print results only for what is called the "univariate" analysis of the data. This is the method taught in most introductory statistics courses. Note that an alternative method for doing the calculations for repeated measures ANOVA, called the "multivariate approach," is an advanced topic rarely covered in introductory courses. To obtain the multivariate results, merely omit the **/PRINT SIGNIF (AVONLY)** subcommand. We must warn you, however, that you will be inundated with a lot of output that you probably won't understand. Also note that if your within-subjects variable has only two levels, then the univariate and multivariate procedures are identical and so only the univariate results are printed. In this case, it is not necessary to include the **/PRINT SIGNIF (AVONLY)** subcommand, although it is probably a good idea to get into the habit of including it anyway.

The **/OMEANS** (observed means) subcommand tells SPSS/PC+ to produce the observed means for each level of the within-subjects factor (for each dependent variable listed in the **MANOVA** command).

The **/DESIGN** subcommand tells SPSS/PC+ to run the analysis according to the requested specifications. It tells SPSS/PC+ to go ahead and produce all requested output (significance tests and observed means). The **/DESIGN** subcommand must always be the last specification on the **MANOVA** command line.

```
       20 cases accepted.
        0 cases rejected because of out-of-range factor values.
        0 cases rejected because of missing data.
        1 non-empty cells.

        1 design will be processed.

- - - - - - - - - - -

Cell Means and Standard Deviations

Variable .. BASELINE
                                                 Mean  Std. Dev.         N

For entire sample                              84.900      7.511        20


Variable .. MEDITATE
                                                 Mean  Std. Dev.         N

For entire sample                              73.600      6.969        20


Variable .. COMEDY
                                                 Mean  Std. Dev.         N

For entire sample                              78.650      7.036        20


Variable .. NATURE
                                                 Mean  Std. Dev.         N

For entire sample                              74.650      7.006        20


Variable .. MUSIC
                                                 Mean  Std. Dev.         N

For entire sample                              77.700      7.420        20
```

```
. . . . . . . . . . . . . . . . . . . . . . . . . . . . . . . . . . . . . . . .

* * ANALYSIS  OF  VARIANCE - DESIGN   1 * *

Tests of Between-Subjects Effects.

 AVERAGED Tests of Significance for MEAS.1 using UNIQUE sums of squares
 Source of Variation           SS      DF        MS          F  Sig of F

 WITHIN CELLS             4787.00      19    251.95
 CONSTANT               606841.00       1 606841.00    2408.60      .000

 - - - - - - - - - -

. . . . . . . . . . . . . . . . . . . . . . . . . . . . . . . . . . . . . . . .

* * ANALYSIS  OF  VARIANCE - DESIGN   1 * *

Tests involving 'COND' Within-Subject Effect.

 AVERAGED Tests of Significance for MEAS.1 using UNIQUE sums of squares
 Source of Variation           SS      DF        MS          F  Sig of F

 WITHIN CELLS              126.90      76      1.67
 COND                     1573.10       4    393.27     235.53      .000

 - - - - - - - - - -

. . . . . . . . . . . . . . . . . . . . . . . . . . . . . . . . . . . . . . . .
```

When you execute the **MANOVA** command, the **/OMEANS** output appears first. The mean, standard deviation, and sample size are given for each dependent variable—that is, for each level of the within-subjects factor.

When you conduct a repeated measures analysis in SPSS/PC+, a CONSTANT effect is automatically tested. You can disregard this part of the output because it is irrelevant for most purposes.

Next, SPSS/PC+ produces a significance test of the null hypothesis that there are no differences in the average heart rates for the five conditions. The sums of squares ("SS"), degrees of freedom ("DF"), and mean squares ("MS") are given for the treatment condition ("COND") and for the error term ("WITHIN CELLS"). Although the error term is labeled "WITHIN CELLS," it actually represents the interaction of treatments by subjects. Therefore, its degrees of freedom equal the product of the number of subjects (20) minus one and the number of levels (5) minus one. The degrees of freedom for COND (treatment) is equal to the number of levels (5) minus one.

In this example, the resulting *F* ratio is 235.53, and its associated *p*-value, printed under "Sig of F," is less than .0005. (Remember, a *p*-value printed as ".000" has just been rounded off.) The null hypothesis is rejected; condition does appear to have an effect on measured heart rates.

As with the between-groups ANOVA discussed previously, it is often appropriate to conduct additional analyses to examine in greater detail which conditions differ from which other conditions. Procedures for both planned comparisons (contrasts) and post hoc tests are available for within-subjects designs, just as they are for between-groups designs. However, these procedures are beyond the scope of this manual.

# Two-Way Mixed ANOVA

## Sample Problem

An adult attachment researcher read an article about the effects of insecure attachment on the physiology of sleep in children. This researcher found the results to be very compelling and hypothesized that similar effects may be observed in romantic couples. Therefore, he conducted a similar study in order to empirically demonstrate the effects of secure romantic attachment on the physiology of sleep. Previous research indicated that periods of almost any kind of anxiety or stress are associated with sleep disturbances, such as a reduction in the time spent in deep (delta) sleep; individuals who are stressed exhibit a tendency toward less and lighter sleep. For this study, the researcher wanted to determine whether the presence of a romantic partner while sleeping reduces sleep disturbances in individuals who are stressed. Thirty women who recently moved to a new area to begin new jobs and their romantic partners were selected for participation in the study. The sleep patterns of ten secure, ten anxious, and ten avoidant women were monitored while they slept alone and while they slept with their romantic partners. Of primary importance to the attachment researcher was the overall percentage of time that each woman spent in deep delta sleep. The investigator hypothesized that all the women will experience sleep disturbances in the absence of their romantic partners due to the stressful nature of their present circumstances. However, it was hypothesized that women with secure attachment styles will derive comfort from the presence of their romantic partners and will sleep better (experience more delta sleep) than women with insecure attachment styles. The table lists the average amounts of time that each woman spent in delta sleep in each partner-proximity condition, expressed as a percentage of total sleep time.

| *Subject* | *Attachment Style** | *Partner-Absent Delta* | *Partner-Present Delta* |
|---|---|---|---|
| 1 | 1 | 17 | 22 |
| 2 | 1 | 16 | 25 |
| 3 | 1 | 15 | 21 |
| 4 | 1 | 18 | 23 |
| 5 | 1 | 19 | 22 |
| 6 | 1 | 20 | 25 |
| 7 | 1 | 17 | 22 |
| 8 | 1 | 15 | 21 |
| 9 | 1 | 16 | 23 |
| 10 | 1 | 15 | 22 |

| *Subject* | *Attachment Style** | *Partner-Absent Delta* | *Partner-Present Delta* |
|---|---|---|---|
| 11 | 2 | 14 | 15 |
| 12 | 2 | 15 | 17 |
| 13 | 2 | 17 | 17 |
| 14 | 2 | 19 | 20 |
| 15 | 2 | 15 | 18 |
| 16 | 2 | 14 | 15 |
| 17 | 2 | 15 | 14 |
| 18 | 2 | 13 | 15 |
| 19 | 2 | 15 | 14 |
| 20 | 2 | 15 | 16 |
| 21 | 3 | 19 | 20 |
| 22 | 3 | 15 | 15 |
| 23 | 3 | 15 | 15 |
| 24 | 3 | 17 | 18 |
| 25 | 3 | 18 | 18 |
| 26 | 3 | 19 | 19 |
| 27 | 3 | 15 | 16 |
| 28 | 3 | 15 | 17 |
| 29 | 3 | 17 | 15 |
| 30 | 3 | 16 | 16 |

*For attachment style: 1 = secure, 2 = anxious, 3 = avoidant.

In this example, we are conducting a two-way mixed analysis of variance with one within-subjects factor and one between-groups factor. Partner proximity is a within-subjects factor because each woman's sleep patterns were monitored both in the presence and in the absence of her romantic partner. Attachment style is a between-groups factor because it subdivides the sample into three discrete subgroups; each subject has only one attachment style: secure, anxious, or avoidant.

As in any two-way analysis of variance, three different null hypotheses (two main effects and an interaction) are tested. The three null hypotheses that we are testing in this problem are as follows:

1. There is no main effect of attachment style: There is no difference in the mean percentages of delta sleep for the three populations of secure, anxious, and avoidant women.

2. There is no main effect of partner proximity: There is no difference in the mean percentages of delta sleep for women in the two partner-proximity conditions. Women spend an equal percentage of time in delta sleep when their romantic partners are present and when they are absent.

3. There is no interaction (attachment style × partner proximity): The effect of attachment style is independent of partner proximity. The effects of the factor attachment style are consistent for both levels of the factor partner proximity.

## *Analysis*

```
DATA LIST FIXED / SUBJECT 1-2 ATTSTYLE 4 PADELTA 6-7 PPDELTA 9-10.
BEGIN DATA.
 1 1 17 22
 2 1 16 25
 3 1 15 21
 4 1 18 23
 5 1 19 22
 6 1 20 25
 7 1 17 22
 8 1 15 21
 9 1 16 23
10 1 15 22
11 2 14 15
12 2 15 17
13 2 17 17
14 2 19 20
15 2 15 18
16 2 14 15
17 2 15 14
18 2 13 15
19 2 15 14
20 2 15 16
21 3 19 20
22 3 15 15
23 3 15 15
24 3 17 18
25 3 18 18
26 3 19 19
27 3 15 16
28 3 15 17
29 3 17 15
30 3 16 16
END DATA.
MANOVA PADELTA PPDELTA BY ATTSTYLE (1,3)
       /WSFACTORS PARTNER (2)
       /OMEANS
       /DESIGN.
```

The **MANOVA** (multivariate analysis of variance) command in SPSS/PC+ can be used to conduct a wide variety of univariate as well as multivariate (those with several dependent variables) analyses. Here, we are using the **MANOVA** command to conduct a two-way mixed analysis of variance. The commands are similar to those used in the one-way within-subjects ANOVA, except that we are adding a between-subjects factor to the analysis.

Because we are conducting a repeated measures analysis, we must set up our data so that the repeated measurements (partner-absent delta and partner-present delta) are different variables. Notice that, although we are measuring the same thing (percentage of time spent in delta sleep) for each woman under both partner-proximity conditions, the data values are entered as if there were two separate dependent measures. Each dependent variable represents a different level of the within-subjects factor (partner proximity).

After the **MANOVA** command, you must type the names of the dependent variables that describe each partner-proximity condition. In this example, our variable names are PADELTA and PPDELTA (for partner-absent delta and partner-present delta). Each dependent variable listed represents delta sleep measured at different times for the same woman.

Next, because we also have a between-subjects factor (or grouping variable), we must type the word BY followed by the name of that factor. In this example, the name of our grouping variable is ATTSTYLE. After typing the name of the grouping variable, we must type, in parentheses, the value of its lowest code, a comma, and then the value of its highest code. In this example, the grouping variable ATTSTYLE is followed by **(1,3)**, which identifies the minimum and maximum values for the three levels of this factor: 1 = secure, 2 = anxious, 3 = avoidant.

The subcommand **/WSFACTORS** (within-subjects factors) must be the first subcommand typed after the variable names. Then you must type a name for your within-subjects factor. This *cannot* be the name of one of your existing variables. In this example, we chose the name PARTNER to indicate that we are measuring the effects of two partner-proximity conditions. Next, you must type, in parentheses, the number of levels for the within-subjects factor. In this example, there are **(2)** levels of our within-subjects factor PARTNER. (This tells SPSS/PC+ that we do not really have two separate dependent variables. We have two levels of one dependent variable called PARTNER.)

The **/OMEANS** (observed means) subcommand tells SPSS/PC+ to produce the observed means of the dependent variables (of each level of the within-subjects factor) listed in the **MANOVA** command for each level of the grouping variable ATTSTYLE.

The **/DESIGN** subcommand tells SPSS/PC+ to run the analysis according to the requested specifications. It tells SPSS/PC+ to go ahead and produce all requested output (significance tests and observed means). The **/DESIGN** subcommand must always be the last specification in the **MANOVA** command line.

Although we have not done so here, it is a good idea to also add the subcommand **/PRINT SIGNIF (AVONLY)**, as explained in the preceding section on within-subject designs. This will suppress the printing of "multivariate" tests of your within-subjects effects. These tests represent an alternative and much more complex way of testing within-subjects effects, and you probably don't want these results cluttering your output. In this example, our within-subjects factor has only two levels (PARTNER = 1 or 2), and it turns out that the multivariate and "univariate" tests are equivalent when this is the case. Under these conditions, SPSS/PC+ prints only the univariate tests, which are the ones you probably want.

```
* * * * * * * * * * * * * * * * * * * * * * * * * * * * * * * * * * * * * * * * * * * *

       30 cases accepted.
        0 cases rejected because of out-of-range factor values.
        0 cases rejected because of missing data.
        3 non-empty cells.

        1 design will be processed.

 - - - - - - - - - -

Cell Means and Standard Deviations
Variable .. PADELTA
     FACTOR           CODE              Mean  Std. Dev.          N

 ATTSTYLE               1             16.800      1.751         10
 ATTSTYLE               2             15.200      1.687         10
 ATTSTYLE               3             16.600      1.647         10
For entire sample                     16.200      1.789         30

* * * * * * * * * * * * * * * * * * * * * * * * * * * * * * * * * * * * * * * * * * * *

Cell Means and Standard Deviations  (CONT.)
Variable .. PPDELTA
     FACTOR           CODE              Mean  Std. Dev.          N

 ATTSTYLE               1             22.600      1.430         10
 ATTSTYLE               2             16.100      1.912         10
 ATTSTYLE               3             16.900      1.792         10
For entire sample                     18.533      3.381         30

* * * * * * * * * * * * * * * * * * * * * * * * * * * * * * * * * * * * * * * * * * * *
```

```
* * ANALYSIS  OF  VARIANCE – DESIGN   1 * *

Tests of Between-Subjects Effects.

 Tests of Significance for T1 using UNIQUE sums of squares
 Source of Variation             SS       DF          MS          F   Sig of F

 WITHIN CELLS                133.50       27        4.94
 CONSTANT                  18096.07        1    18096.07    3659.88       .000
 ATTSTYLE                    175.43        2       87.72      17.74       .000
```

```
* * ANALYSIS  OF  VARIANCE – DESIGN   1 * *

Tests involving 'DELTA' Within-Subject Effect.

 Tests of Significance for T2 using UNIQUE sums of squares
 Source of Variation             SS       DF          MS          F   Sig of F

 WITHIN CELLS                 24.30       27         .90
 PARTNER                      81.67        1       81.67      90.74       .000
 ATTSTYLE BY PARTNER          91.03        2       45.52      50.57       .000
```

The output for this analysis looks similar to that for the one-way repeated measures ANOVA, except that, in addition to a significance test of the within-subjects factor, significance tests of the between-subjects factor and the interaction of the within- and between-subjects factors are produced.

When you execute the **MANOVA** command, the **/OMEANS** output appears first. The cell means, standard deviations, and sample sizes for each level of the grouping variable ATTSTYLE are given for each level of the within-subjects factor (PADELTA and PPDELTA).

As in our previous example of a two-way between-subjects ANOVA, it is helpful to arrange the cell means into a two-way table:

| PARTNER | | *ATTSTYLE* | | | |
|---|---|---|---|---|---|
| | | *1 = Secure* | *2 = Anxious* | *3 = Avoidant* | |
| | *1 = Absent* | 16.80 | 15.20 | 16.60 | 16.20 |
| | *2 = Present* | 22.60 | 16.10 | 16.90 | 18.53 |
| | | 19.70 | 15.65 | 16.75 | |

Again, the cell means were taken directly from the printout; the "marginal means" were computed by us, by hand, as the mean of the means across cells in a given row or column of the table.

When mixed-model ANOVAs are run in SPSS/PC+, the resulting ANOVA summary table is split into two tables. The first table reports results for the "Between-Subjects Effects," which means all effects that involve only between-subjects independent variables. In this case, the only such effects are those for CONSTANT—which, as in previous analyses, can be safely ignored—and for the main effect of ATTSTYLE. The row labeled "WITHIN CELLS" refers to the error term used to test the between-subjects effects. For each source, sum of squares ("SS"), the degrees of freedom ("DF"), and mean square ("MS") are listed. In this case, the *F* value for ATTSTYLE equals 17.74, with a *p*-value ("Sig of F," reported as ".000") less than .0005. The main effect for ATTSTYLE is significant.

The second table reports the "Within-Subject Effect," which includes the main effect for PARTNER and the ATTSTYLE BY PARTNER interaction. The line labeled "WITHIN CELLS" represents the error term used to test these two effects. Note that this is different from the error term used for testing the between-subjects effects in the previous table. The remainder of the table follows the same format as the previous table. Both the main effect for PARTNER and the ATTSTYLE BY PARTNER interaction have *p*-values ("Sig of F") less than .0005 (reported as ".000) and are significant.

• • • • • •

# Correlations

## Sample Problem

An aerobics instructor believes that, aside from the physical benefits of exercising, such as muscle tone, low body fat, weight control, there are also numerous mental/psychological advantages to engaging in a regular aerobic exercise program. She believes that regular aerobic exercise is related to greater mental acuity, stress reduction, high self-esteem, and greater overall life satisfaction. In order to test this hypothesis, she recruits a random sample of 30 adults to participate in her study. Each subject is asked to fill out the following questionnaires: (1) a preliminary questionnaire asking subjects to report the average number of hours per week they engage in some sort of aerobic exercise; (2) a self-esteem scale (higher scores indicate greater self-esteem); (3) a life satisfaction questionnaire to determine each subject's overall outlook on life (higher scores indicate greater life satisfaction); (4) a perceived stress questionnaire, in which subjects are asked to read a series of vignettes describing potentially stressful events and are asked to rate the degree to which they perceive each event as stressful (higher scores indicate greater stress); and (5) an intelligence test to determine the IQ of each subject. The results are listed in the table.

| *Subject* | *Exercise* | *Self-Esteem* | *Satisfaction* | *Stress* | *IQ* |
|---|---|---|---|---|---|
| 1 | 10 | 25 | 45 | 20 | 105 |
| 2 | 33 | 37 | 40 | 10 | 120 |
| 3 | 9 | 12 | 30 | 13 | 110 |
| 4 | 14 | 32 | 39 | 15 | 100 |
| 5 | 3 | 22 | 27 | 29 | 105 |
| 6 | 12 | 31 | 44 | 22 | 120 |
| 7 | 7 | 30 | 39 | 13 | 110 |
| 8 | 15 | 30 | 40 | 20 | 110 |
| 9 | 3 | 15 | 46 | 25 | 95 |
| 10 | 21 | 34 | 50 | 10 | 125 |
| 11 | 2 | 18 | 29 | 33 | 105 |
| 12 | 20 | 37 | 47 | 5 | 105 |
| 13 | 4 | 19 | 31 | 23 | 100 |
| 14 | 8 | 33 | 38 | 21 | 105 |
| 15 | 0 | 10 | 25 | 30 | 100 |
| 16 | 17 | 35 | 42 | 13 | 105 |
| 17 | 25 | 39 | 40 | 10 | 110 |
| 18 | 2 | 13 | 30 | 27 | 105 |

| *Subject* | *Exercise* | *Self-Esteem* | *Satisfaction* | *Stress* | *IQ* |
|---|---|---|---|---|---|
| 19 | 18 | 35 | 47 | 9 | 105 |
| 20 | 3 | 15 | 28 | 25 | 100 |
| 21 | 27 | 35 | 39 | 7 | 115 |
| 22 | 4 | 17 | 32 | 34 | 115 |
| 23 | 8 | 20 | 34 | 20 | 110 |
| 24 | 10 | 22 | 41 | 15 | 95 |
| 25 | 0 | 14 | 27 | 35 | 105 |
| 26 | 12 | 35 | 35 | 20 | 115 |
| 27 | 5 | 20 | 30 | 23 | 105 |
| 28 | 7 | 29 | 30 | 12 | 95 |
| 29 | 30 | 40 | 48 | 14 | 110 |
| 30 | 14 | 30 | 45 | 15 | 110 |

In this problem, we are interested in calculating the Pearson product-moment correlation between each pair of variables. In addition, for each pair, we wish to test the null hypothesis that the correlation between the variables in the population from which the sample was drawn equals zero.

## Analysis

```
DATA LIST FIXED / SUBJECT 1-2 EXERCISE 4-5 ESTEEM 7-8 SATISFY 10-11
                  STRESS 13-14 IQ 16-18.
BEGIN DATA.
 1 10 25 45 20 105
 2 33 37 40 10 120
 3  9 12 30 13 110
 4 14 32 39 15 100
 5  3 22 27 29 105
 6 12 31 44 22 120
 7  7 30 39 13 110
 8 15 30 40 20 110
 9  3 15 46 25  95
10 21 34 50 10 125
11  2 18 29 33 105
12 20 37 47  5 105
13  4 19 31 23 100
14  8 33 38 21 105
15  0 10 25 30 100
16 17 35 42 13 105
17 25 39 40 10 110
```

```
18  2 13 30 27 105
19 18 35 47  9 105
20  3 15 28 25 100
21 27 35 39  7 115
22  4 17 32 34 115
23  8 20 34 20 110
24 10 22 41 15  95
25  0 14 27 35 105
26 12 35 35 20 115
27  5 20 30 23 105
28  7 29 30 12  95
29 30 40 48 14 110
30 14 30 45 15 110
END DATA.
CORRELATIONS /VARIABLES EXERCISE ESTEEM SATISFY STRESS IQ
             /STATISTICS 1.
```

The **CORRELATIONS** command is used to calculate the Pearson correlation coefficients between pairs of variables.

After the **CORRELATIONS** command, you must type the subcommand **/VARIABLES**, and then type the names of the variables to be correlated. In this example, we want to correlate the variables EXERCISE, ESTEEM, SATISFY, STRESS, and IQ.

*Important note:* In SPSS/PC+ Version 5.0, these commands will produce two-tailed (nondirectional) significance tests, as illustrated in the output that follows. To obtain one-tailed tests instead, you must also specify **/OPTIONS 3**. SPSS/PC+ Version 4.0 is exactly the opposite: The commands listed at the beginning of this section will produce one-tailed (directional) significance tests, and the additional subcommand **/OPTIONS 3** is required if you wish to obtain two-tailed tests instead.

By default, SPSS/PC+ will simply indicate which correlations are statistically significant, at various alpha levels, using asterisks. To obtain exact *p*-values, specify **/OPTIONS 5**. (To specify both this and option 3, use **/OPTIONS 3,5**.)

The **/STATISTICS 1** subcommand requests additional descriptive statistics for each variable and is optional.

```
Variable      Cases           Mean           Std Dev

EXERCISE         30        11.4333            9.0580
ESTEEM           30        26.1333            9.2242
SATISFY          30        37.2667            7.3949
STRESS           30        18.9333            8.2960
IQ               30       107.1667            7.3910
```

```
Correlations:  EXERCISE    ESTEEM      SATISFY     STRESS      IQ

  EXERCISE    1.0000      .8433**     .6777**    -.7884**     .5237*
  ESTEEM       .8433**   1.0000       .7011**    -.7466**     .4230
  SATISFY      .6777**    .7011**    1.0000      -.6489**     .3108
  STRESS      -.7884**   -.7466**    -.6489**    1.0000      -.2253
  IQ           .5237*     .4230       .3108      -.2253      1.0000

N of cases:    30          2-tailed Signif:  * - .01   ** - .001

" . " is printed if a coefficient cannot be computed
```

When you execute the **CORRELATIONS** command, the descriptive statistics for each variable (if requested) are produced first.

Next, SPSS/PC+ produces a correlation matrix that shows the correlations between all possible pairs of variables and indicates the number of cases used to compute them.

The two-tailed significance levels are indicated with asterisks. (*Note:* This is the output produced by SPSS/PC+ Version 4.0 with **/OPTIONS 3** or SPSS/PC+ Version 5.0 without **/OPTIONS 3**. Otherwise, SPSS/PC+ would indicate one-tailed rather than two-tailed significance levels. To be sure, always check your output carefully to see whether it indicates "2-tailed Signif," as in the preceding output, or "1-tailed Signif.") If there are no asterisks following a correlation coefficient, then the correlation between those two variables is not statistically significant. If one asterisk follows a correlation coefficient, then the correlation between those two variables is statistically significant at the .01 significance level (i.e, $p < .01$). If two asterisks follow a correlation coefficient, then the correlation between those two variables is statistically significant at the .001 significance level ($p < .001$).

# Simple Regression

## Sample Problem

A second-grade teacher at Lakewood Elementary School believes that the amount of time parents spend reading to or with their children is a fairly accurate predictor of overall school performance. To test this hypothesis, the teacher conducted a study using the 25 students in his second-grade class. At the end of the school year, each child's letter grades for the entire year were used to calculate an overall grade point average. During a PTA meeting, parents were given a questionnaire on which they were asked to indicate the average amount of time per week (in hours) that they spend reading to or with their children. In order to avoid experimenter bias, the teacher did not look at the questionnaires until after he graded and calculated the grade point averages for his students. The results are listed in the table.

| *Child* | *Reading Time* (X) | *GPA* (Y) |
|---|---|---|
| 1 | 2 | 2.12 |
| 2 | 5 | 3.00 |
| 3 | 15 | 4.00 |
| 4 | 1 | 2.00 |
| 5 | 3 | 2.56 |
| 6 | 0 | 1.73 |
| 7 | 7 | 3.91 |
| 8 | 12 | 3.77 |
| 9 | 2 | 2.12 |
| 10 | 6 | 3.55 |
| 11 | 10 | 3.85 |
| 12 | 8 | 3.12 |
| 13 | 5 | 3.68 |
| 14 | 2 | 2.22 |
| 15 | 7 | 3.50 |
| 16 | 0 | 1.68 |
| 17 | 14 | 4.00 |
| 18 | 7 | 3.86 |
| 19 | 9 | 4.00 |
| 20 | 1 | 1.84 |
| 21 | 5 | 3.50 |
| 22 | 7 | 3.70 |
| 23 | 4 | 3.33 |
| 24 | 10 | 3.88 |
| 25 | 3 | 2.98 |

In this example, we wish to (1) find the equation that best represents the linear relationship between the variables *X* and *Y* and that allows us to best predict *Y* scores from *X* scores; (2) determine the strength of this relationship; and (3) test the null hypothesis that, in the population from which the sample was drawn, the slope of the prediction line is 0—that is, *X* scores and *Y* scores are unrelated.

## *Analysis: Simple Regression*

```
DATA LIST FIXED /  CHILD 1-2 TIME 4-5 GPA 7-9 (2).
BEGIN DATA.
 1  2 212
 2  5 300
 3 15 400
 4  1 200
 5  3 256
 6  0 173
 7  7 391
 8 12 377
 9  2 212
10  6 355
11 10 385
12  8 312
13  5 368
14  2 222
15  7 350
16  0 168
17 14 400
18  7 386
19  9 400
20  1 184
21  5 350
22  7 370
23  4 333
24 10 388
25  3 298
END DATA.
REGRESSION /DESCRIPTIVES
           /DEPENDENT GPA
           /METHOD ENTER TIME.
```

The **REGRESSION** command is used to produce both simple and multiple regression equations and associated statistics. Multiple regression, in which multiple predictor variables are used simultaneously, is covered in the next section.

The **/DESCRIPTIVES** subcommand tells SPSS/PC+ to produce descriptive statistics for all the variables included in the analysis. These statistics include means, standard deviations, and a correlation matrix.

The **/DEPENDENT** subcommand is used to identify the dependent variable in the regression equation. In this example, our dependent variable is GPA.

The **/METHOD** subcommand must immediately follow the **/DEPENDENT** subcommand. The **/METHOD** subcommand is used to tell SPSS/PC+ the way you want your independent variable(s) to be added to the regression equation. **ENTER** is the most direct method used to build a regression equation; it tells SPSS/PC+ to enter all the independent variable(s) that you indicate for inclusion in the regression equation. In this example, the independent variable is TIME.

```
  * * * *   M U L T I P L E   R E G R E S S I O N   * * * *

Listwise Deletion of Missing Data

             Mean  Std Dev  Label

GPA         3.116     .823
TIME        5.800    4.203

N of Cases =     25

Correlation:

                 GPA        TIME

GPA            1.000        .860
TIME            .860       1.000
```

```
  * * * *   M U L T I P L E   R E G R E S S I O N   * * * *

Equation Number 1    Dependent Variable..   GPA

Block Number  1.  Method:  Enter      TIME

Variable(s) Entered on Step Number
   1..    TIME
```

```
Multiple R           .85978
R Square             .73922
Adjusted R Square    .72788
Standard Error       .42926

Analysis of Variance
                     DF      Sum of Squares      Mean Square
Regression            1            12.01339         12.01339
Residual             23             4.23801           .18426

F =       65.19755        Signif F =  .0000
```

. . . . . . . . . . . . . . . . . . . . . . . . . . . . . . . . . . . . . . . . . . . .

```
  * * * *  M U L T I P L E   R E G R E S S I O N   * * * *

Equation Number 1    Dependent Variable..   GPA


------------------ Variables in the Equation ------------------

Variable               B          SE B        Beta          T  Sig T

TIME             .168325       .020847     .859780      8.075  .0000
(Constant)      2.139712       .148289                 14.429  .0000


End Block Number   1   All requested variables entered.
```

. . . . . . . . . . . . . . . . . . . . . . . . . . . . . . . . . . . . . . . . . . . .

When you execute the **REGRESSION** command, the descriptive statistics are produced first. The means, standard deviations, number of cases, and a correlation matrix are given for the two variables GPA and TIME. The correlation between these two variables is .860, which indicates that there is a strong positive relationship: Children whose parents spend more time reading to or with them tend to perform better in school. (*Note:* Although the matrix includes four values, there is really only one meaningful correlation; the correlation of each variable with itself must be 1.0, and the correlation of GPA with TIME must be identical to the correlation of TIME with GPA. This is the same correlation coefficient that would be produced by the **CORRELATIONS** command.)

Next, SPSS/PC+ produces regression statistics including Multiple R, R Square, Adjusted R Square, and the Standard Error of the estimate. It is interesting to note that in simple regression, in which only one predictor variable is used, the Multiple R is equivalent to the simple correlation between the predictor and dependent variables (in this case, .860).

An ANOVA table for the regression equation is produced next; this represents a test of the null hypothesis that *R*-squared in the population equals 0. The variance of the dependent variable is partitioned into two sources: the part predictable from the regression equation ("Regression") and the part not predictable from the equation ("Residual," or error). The *F* test is significant. Two interesting things to note here are: (1) the sum of squares regression divided by the sum of squares total (that is, regression plus residual) equals *R*-squared, and thus the proportion of variance in the dependent variable that is predictable from the independent variable; and (2) the significance test for *R*-squared, when there is only one predictor variable, is equivalent to a simple test of the correlation between the independent and dependent variables.

The final section of the output provides the information needed to construct a least-squares regression (prediction) line. The column labeled "B" lists the regression coefficients for the independent variable TIME and for the "Constant" term. These represent the slope and *Y*-intercept, respectively, for the regression equation. Thus, in this example, the least-squares prediction equation is

$$\text{Predicted GPA} = 2.14 + (.168325)(\text{TIME})$$

The values listed under "Beta" are an alternative set of coefficients that would be used if all variables were first converted to *Z*-scores—that is, "standardized." Note that there is no value for "Constant" in this column. If both variables are in *Z*-score form, then the *Y*-intercept will always be 0. Thus, the prediction equation for predicting *Z*-scores on *Y* from *Z*-scores on *X* is

$$\text{Predicted } Z_{GPA} = 0 + (.859780)(Z_{TIME})$$

The last two columns in the output report the results of the significance tests for the coefficients. The null hypotheses being tested are, respectively, (1) that the *B* coefficient in the population equals 0, and (2) that the *Y*-intercept in the population equals 0. The *t*- and *p*-values are labeled "T" and "Sig T," respectively. Both *p*-values are reported as ".0000," which in this case means that the actual *p*-values are less than .00005 and are rounded off. Both coefficients are significantly different from 0.

## *Analysis: Scatterplots*

We can also use SPSS/PC+ to generate a graph (scatterplot) of our data (showing the regression line) for descriptive purposes. We have not reprinted the **DATA LIST** command and data here. To create a scatterplot corresponding to the preceding analysis, simply use the following command instead of or in addition to the previous **REGRESSION** command:

```
PLOT /FORMAT REGRESSION /PLOT GPA WITH TIME.
```

The subcommand **/FORMAT REGRESSION** is used to produce regression plots and statistics. This subcommand tells SPSS/PC+ to place the letter R on the graph to indicate where the regression line should be drawn. This subcommand also tells SPSS/PC+ to produce regression statistics. If this subcommand is omitted, only the scatterplot will be produced.

The subcommand **/PLOT** must be used to tell SPSS/PC+ which variables to plot. (*Note:* This must be the last subcommand in the **PLOT** command.) After the subcommand **/PLOT**, you must type the name of your dependent variable. This variable will be plotted on the vertical axis of the scatterplot. In this example, our dependent variable is GPA. Then, you must type the keyword **WITH**, followed by the name of your independent variable. This variable will be plotted on the horizontal axis of the scatterplot. In this example, our independent variable is TIME.

If you type more than one variable name on either side of the keyword **WITH**, SPSS/PC+ will produce a scatterplot for every combination of vertical-axis variables and horizontal-axis variables.

```
. . . . . . . . . . . . . . . . . . . . . . . . . . . . . . . . . . . . . . . . . . . . . . . . . . . . . . .

* * * * * * * * * * * * * * *   P  L  O  T   * * * * * * * * * * * * * *

Data    Information

        25 unweighted cases accepted.

. . . . . . . . . . . . . . . . . . . . . . . . . . . . . . . . . . . . . . . . . . . . . . . . . . . . . . .
```

PLOT OF GPA WITH TIME

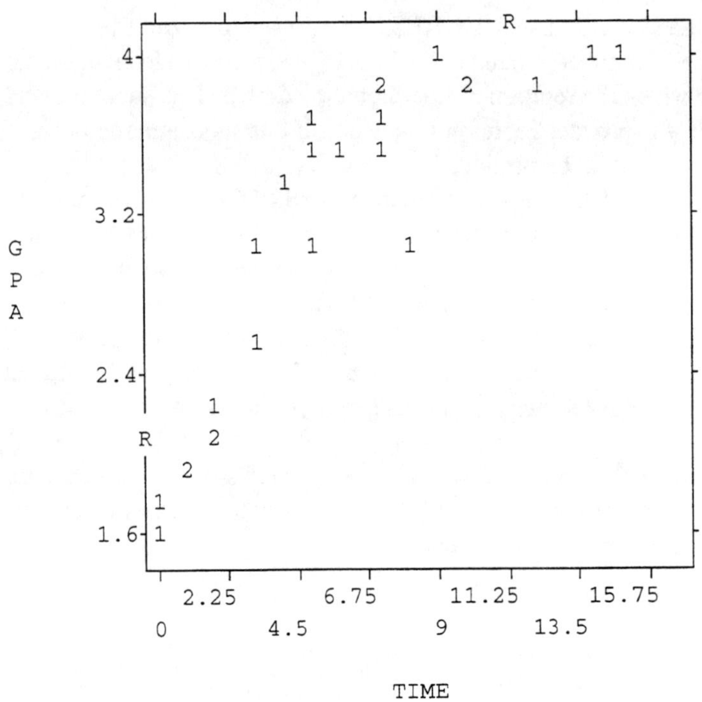


```
. . . . . . . . . . . . . . . . . . . . . . . . . . . . . . . . . . . . . . . . . . . . . . . . . . . . . . .

25 cases plotted. Regression statistics of GPA on TIME:
Correlation  .85978 R Squared   .73922  S.E. of Est   .42926 Sig.   .0000
Intercept(S.E.)     2.13971(    .14829)  Slope(S.E.)   .16833(    .02085)

. . . . . . . . . . . . . . . . . . . . . . . . . . . . . . . . . . . . . . . . . . . . . . . . . . . . . . .
```

When you execute the **PLOT** command, SPSS/PC+ produces a scatterplot of GPA with TIME. The independent variable (TIME) is located on the horizontal axis, and the dependent variable (GPA) is located on the vertical axis. The 1's and 2's on the graph indicate the location of each plot and the number of cases (subjects) that occupy that particular location.

In addition, SPSS/PC+ prints the letter R on the frame of the graph to indicate where the regression (prediction) line should be drawn. You can see the location of the regression line by using a ruler to draw a straight line between the two R's.

Next, regression statistics are produced, including the correlation coefficient, *R*-squared, standard error of the estimate, and *p*-value for the test of the null hypothesis that the population *R*-squared is equal to 0. The values of the intercept and slope, along with their estimated standard errors, are also given. These values are identical to those generated by the **REGRESSION** command, although they are presented in a less convenient and readable format by the **PLOT** command.

• • • • • •

# *Multiple Regression*

## *Sample Problem*

A resilience researcher conducted a study with an "at risk" preschool population in a continuing effort to determine why many children who grow up in potentially damaging environments come through relatively unharmed and well adjusted while other children succumb to the stress. This preschool population was deemed to be "at risk" for educational and developmental delays because of a number of risk factors including low social status, parental psychiatric disorders or criminality, and overcrowding/large families. Because past resilience research suggests that family social support, child biological dispositions (temperament), and characteristics of the home environment are associated with the likelihood of future adaptive outcomes, the researcher decided to investigate these variables to determine whether they would be powerful predictors of resilience in a sample of 30 at-risk preschool children. The children were tested for age-appropriate developmental abilities (verbal, motor, cognitive, self-help, emotional, and social), and an aggregate score for these abilities was used as the dependent measure of resilience. (Higher scores indicate greater overall developmental abilities.) Families were asked to fill out a social support questionnaire to measure the helpfulness of sources of support to families raising a young child. (Higher scores indicate greater support.) Teachers were asked to rate aspects of each child's home environment—such as emotional and verbal responsiveness of parents, learning and language stimulation, and availability of play materials—during regular home visits. (Higher scores indicate a more positive home environment.) A child temperament scale was also completed by teachers. (Higher scores indicate an easy, adaptive, flexible temperamental style, and lower scores indicate an intense, difficult, less malleable temperamental style.) The results are listed in the table.

| *Child* | *Social Support* | *Temperament* | *Home Environment* | *Development* |
|---|---|---|---|---|
| 1 | 37 | 21 | 20 | 25 |
| 2 | 85 | 38 | 25 | 48 |
| 3 | 43 | 18 | 19 | 22 |
| 4 | 68 | 37 | 27 | 49 |
| 5 | 30 | 12 | 18 | 15 |
| 6 | 57 | 33 | 23 | 37 |
| 7 | 87 | 38 | 29 | 60 |
| 8 | 15 | 35 | 22 | 30 |
| 9 | 72 | 41 | 36 | 55 |

| *Child* | *Social Support* | *Temperament* | *Home Environment* | *Development* |
|---|---|---|---|---|
| 10 | 40 | 35 | 21 | 27 |
| 11 | 60 | 34 | 20 | 47 |
| 12 | 54 | 29 | 26 | 43 |
| 13 | 79 | 31 | 35 | 50 |
| 14 | 56 | 32 | 28 | 45 |
| 15 | 35 | 25 | 29 | 27 |
| 16 | 53 | 28 | 24 | 39 |
| 17 | 75 | 39 | 31 | 52 |
| 18 | 70 | 35 | 26 | 53 |
| 19 | 79 | 31 | 24 | 60 |
| 20 | 31 | 42 | 19 | 20 |
| 21 | 17 | 40 | 22 | 32 |
| 22 | 82 | 41 | 31 | 58 |
| 23 | 59 | 40 | 27 | 41 |
| 24 | 26 | 25 | 15 | 17 |
| 25 | 54 | 39 | 24 | 33 |
| 26 | 27 | 19 | 19 | 20 |
| 27 | 62 | 45 | 29 | 44 |
| 28 | 79 | 47 | 28 | 56 |
| 29 | 26 | 30 | 10 | 18 |
| 30 | 69 | 33 | 29 | 59 |

In multiple regression analysis a dependent variable (in this case, developmental ability) is predicted from several independent variables simultaneously. As in simple regression, however, we are interested in determining (1) the equation for best predicting the dependent variable from a linear combination of predictors and (2) how well this "best" equation does in fact predict variability in the dependent variable. In addition, we are generally interested in significance tests to assess the contributions of each of the variables to the prediction equation.

## *Analysis*

```
DATA LIST FIXED / SUBJECT 1-2 SUPPORT 4-5 TEMPER 7-8 HOMEENV 10-11
                  DEVELOP 13-14.
BEGIN DATA.
 1 37 21 20 25
 2 85 38 25 48
 3 43 18 19 22
 4 68 37 27 49
 5 30 12 18 15
 6 57 33 23 37
 7 87 38 29 60
```

```
 8 15 35 22 30
 9 72 41 36 55
10 40 35 21 27
11 60 34 20 47
12 54 29 26 43
13 79 31 35 50
14 56 32 28 45
15 35 25 29 27
16 53 28 24 39
17 75 39 31 52
18 70 35 26 53
19 79 31 24 60
20 31 42 19 20
21 17 40 22 32
22 82 41 31 58
23 59 40 27 41
24 26 25 15 17
25 54 39 24 33
26 27 19 19 20
27 62 45 29 44
28 79 47 28 56
29 26 30 10 18
30 69 33 29 59
END DATA.
REGRESSION /VARIABLES SUPPORT TEMPER HOMEENV DEVELOP
           /DESCRIPTIVES
           /DEPENDENT DEVELOP
           /METHOD ENTER SUPPORT TEMPER HOMEENV.
```

The **REGRESSION** command is used to produce multiple regression equations and associated statistics.

The **/VARIABLES** subcommand is used to specify the names of all the variables (dependent and independent) that we will be using in the analysis. This subcommand is optional because, if it is omitted, SPSS/PC+ produces regression equations and statistics for the variables named in the **/DEPENDENT** and **/METHOD** subcommands by default. Also, because we did name all of our variables in the **/VARIABLES** subcommand, we could have simply typed the word **ENTER** after the **/METHOD** subcommand (without specifying any variable names). In this case, SPSS/PC+ would enter all the variables listed in the **/VARIABLES** subcommand except the dependent variable. The variables that we are using in this analysis are SUPPORT, TEMPER, HOMEENV, and DEVELOP.

The **/DESCRIPTIVES** subcommand tells SPSS/PC+ to produce descriptive statistics for all the variables included in the analysis. These statistics are means, standard deviations, and a correlation matrix.

The **/DEPENDENT** subcommand is used to identify the dependent variable in the regression equation. In this example, our dependent variable is DEVELOP.

The **/METHOD** subcommand must immediately follow the **/DEPENDENT** subcommand. The **/METHOD** subcommand is used to tell SPSS/PC+ the way you want your independent variable(s) to be added to the regression equation. **ENTER** is the most direct method used to build a regression equation; it tells SPSS/PC+ to enter all the independent variable(s) (in a single step) that you indicate for inclusion in the regression equation. In this example, our independent variables are SUPPORT, TEMPER, and HOMEENV.

We should note in passing that the **REGRESSION** command offers a variety of other analysis options as well, including several "stepwise" procedures and the ability to test the contribution to the prediction of several variables jointly. Both of these applications are rather complex and beyond the scope of this manual.

```
          * * * *   M U L T I P L E   R E G R E S S I O N   * * * *

Listwise Deletion of Missing Data

             Mean  Std Dev  Label

SUPPORT    54.233   21.614
TEMPER     33.100    8.285
HOMEENV    24.533    5.728
DEVELOP    39.400   14.576

N of Cases =     30
```

```
Correlation:

             SUPPORT      TEMPER     HOMEENV     DEVELOP

SUPPORT        1.000        .468        .716        .899
TEMPER          .468       1.000        .481        .582
HOMEENV         .716        .481       1.000        .776
DEVELOP         .899        .582        .776       1.000
```

```
. . . . . . . . . . . . . . . . . . . . . . . . . . . . . . . . . . . . . . . . . . . . .

      * * * *   M U L T I P L E   R E G R E S S I O N   * * * *

Equation Number 1    Dependent Variable..   DEVELOP

Block Number  1.  Method:  Enter       SUPPORT  TEMPER   HOMEENV

. . . . . . . . . . . . . . . . . . . . . . . . . . . . . . . . . . . . . . . . . . . . .

      * * * *   M U L T I P L E   R E G R E S S I O N   * * * *

Equation Number 1    Dependent Variable..   DEVELOP

Variable(s) Entered on Step Number
   1..    HOMEENV
   2..    TEMPER
   3..    SUPPORT

Multiple R            .92984
R Square              .86460
Adjusted R Square     .84898
Standard Error       5.66440

Analysis of Variance
                     DF      Sum of Squares      Mean Square
Regression            3          5326.97910       1775.65970
Residual             26           834.22090         32.08542

F =       55.34164        Signif F =  .0000

. . . . . . . . . . . . . . . . . . . . . . . . . . . . . . . . . . . . . . . . . . . . .

      * * * *   M U L T I P L E   R E G R E S S I O N   * * * *

Equation Number 1    Dependent Variable..   DEVELOP

---------- Variables in the Equation ----------

Variable                B          SE B        Beta           T  Sig T

HOMEENV           .563115      .270754     .221290       2.080  .0475
TEMPER            .290840      .147825     .165319       1.967  .0599
SUPPORT           .447427      .071203     .663463       6.284  .0000
(Constant)      -8.307327     5.343705                  -1.555  .1321

End Block Number   1   All requested variables entered.

. . . . . . . . . . . . . . . . . . . . . . . . . . . . . . . . . . . . . . . . . . . . .
```

When you execute the **REGRESSION** command, the descriptive statistics are produced first. The means, standard deviations, number of cases, and a correlation matrix are given for all the variables used in the analysis. In this example, all of our independent variables correlate positively with the dependent variable.

Next, SPSS/PC+ produces regression statistics including Multiple R, R Square, Adjusted R Square, and the Standard Error of Estimate. Unlike simple regression, in which only one predictor variable is used, Multiple R is not equivalent to any of the simple pairwise correlations printed previously.

An ANOVA table for the regression equation is produced next; this represents a test of the null hypothesis that $R$-squared in the population equals 0. The variance of the dependent variable is partitioned into two sources: the part predictable from the regression equation ("Regression") and the part not predictable from the equation ("Residual," or error). The $F$ test is significant. As in simple regression, the sum of squares regression divided by the sum of squares total (that is, Regression plus Residual) equals $R$-squared and thus the proportion of variance in the dependent variable that is predictable from the independent variables. However, in multiple regression, the significance test for $R$-squared is unique; it is not equivalent to any of the tests for the individual predictor variables.

The final section of the output provides the information needed to construct a least-squares regression (prediction) line. The column labeled "B" lists the regression coefficients for each independent variable and for the "Constant" term. Thus, in this example, the least-squares prediction equation is

$$\text{Predicted DEVELOP} = -8.31 + (.563)(\text{HOMEENV}) + (.291)(\text{TEMPER}) + (.447)(\text{SUPPORT})$$

The values listed under "Beta" are an alternative set of coefficients that would be used if all variables were first converted to $Z$-scores—that is, "standardized." Note that there is no value for "Constant" in this column. If all variables are in $Z$-score form, the "$Y$-intercept" will always be 0. Thus, the prediction equation for predicting $Z$-scores on $Y$ from $Z$-scores on the various predictors is

$$\text{Predicted } Z_{\text{DEVELOP}} = 0 + (.221)(Z_{\text{HOMEENV}}) + (.165)(Z_{\text{TEMPER}}) + (.663)(Z_{\text{SUPPORT}})$$

The last two columns in the output report the results of the significance tests for the coefficients. The null hypotheses being tested are, in each case, that the $B$ coefficient in question equals 0 in the population. In this case, the tests for HOMEENV and SUPPORT are significant at the .05 level, but the test for TEMPER is not significant.

# Chi-Square Test of Independence

## Sample Problem

A psychology student intern, who was volunteering at a nursing home to fulfill a requirement for her Psychology of Aging course, noticed that there seemed to be a relationship between how frequently a patient received visitors and how well that patient was treated by the nursing home staff. Therefore, the student decided to test whether there is significant evidence to conclude that frequency of visitors and staff treatment of patients are related. The student used the visitor log book to determine the frequency of visitors for a random sample of 39 patients. She categorized each patient into one of three visitor categories: frequently visited, occasionally visited, or rarely/never visited. She then asked a nursing intern, who did not know the purpose of the study, to rate (based on conversations with the patients and personal observations) how well she thought each patient was being treated by the nursing home staff. Each patient was categorized into one of three treatment categories: excellent/good treatment, fair treatment, or poor treatment. The results are listed in the table.

| *Patient* | *Visitors** | *Treatment*† |
|---|---|---|
| 1 | 1 | 1 |
| 2 | 1 | 1 |
| 3 | 1 | 1 |
| 4 | 1 | 1 |
| 5 | 1 | 1 |
| 6 | 1 | 1 |
| 7 | 1 | 1 |
| 8 | 1 | 1 |
| 9 | 1 | 1 |
| 10 | 1 | 2 |
| 11 | 1 | 2 |
| 12 | 1 | 2 |
| 13 | 1 | 3 |
| 14 | 2 | 1 |
| 15 | 2 | 2 |
| 16 | 2 | 2 |
| 17 | 2 | 2 |
| 18 | 2 | 2 |
| 19 | 2 | 2 |
| 20 | 2 | 2 |

| *Patient* | *Visitors** | *Treatment*[†] |
|---|---|---|
| 21 | 2 | 2 |
| 22 | 2 | 2 |
| 23 | 2 | 2 |
| 24 | 2 | 2 |
| 25 | 2 | 3 |
| 26 | 2 | 3 |
| 27 | 3 | 1 |
| 28 | 3 | 2 |
| 29 | 3 | 3 |
| 30 | 3 | 3 |
| 31 | 3 | 3 |
| 32 | 3 | 3 |
| 33 | 3 | 3 |
| 34 | 3 | 3 |
| 35 | 3 | 3 |
| 36 | 3 | 3 |
| 37 | 3 | 3 |
| 38 | 3 | 3 |
| 39 | 3 | 3 |

*For visitors: 1 = frequent, 2 = occasional, 3 = rarely/never.
†For treatment: 1 = excellent/good, 2 = fair, 3 = poor.

In this problem, we are testing the null hypothesis that the frequency of visitors that patients receive and the treatment of patients by nursing home staff are independent. In other words, there is no relationship between how frequently a patient receives visitors and how well a patient is treated by the nursing home staff.

## Analysis

```
DATA LIST FIXED / PATIENT 1-2 VISITORS 4 TREAT 6.
BEGIN DATA.
 1 1 1
 2 1 1
 3 1 1
 4 1 1
 5 1 1
 6 1 1
 7 1 1
 8 1 1
 9 1 1
10 1 2
```

```
11 1 2
12 1 2
13 1 3
14 2 1
15 2 2
16 2 2
17 2 2
18 2 2
19 2 2
20 2 2
21 2 2
22 2 2
23 2 2
24 2 2
25 2 3
26 2 3
27 3 1
28 3 2
29 3 3
30 3 3
31 3 3
32 3 3
33 3 3
34 3 3
35 3 3
36 3 3
37 3 3
38 3 3
39 3 3
END DATA.
CROSSTABS /TABLES VISITORS BY TREAT
          /STATISTICS CHISQ
          /CELLS COUNT EXPECTED.
```

The **CROSSTABS** command is used to compute cross-tabulations and various measures of association for two or more variables.

The subcommand **/TABLES** is used to specify the cross-tabulation table(s) that you want SPSS/PC+ to produce. After typing **/TABLES**, you must type the name of your "row variable." In this example, our row variable is VISITORS. Each level of the variable VISITORS defines one row of the table: 1 = frequent, 2 = occasional, 3 = rarely/never. Then you must type the word **BY**, followed by the name of your "column variable." In this example, our column variable is

TREAT (for treatment). Each level of the variable TREAT defines one column of the table: 1 = excellent/good, 2 = fair, 3 = poor. (The word **BY** distinguishes your "row variables" from your "column variables." If you typed more than one row and column variable, SPSS/PC+ would produce a table for every possible pair of a row variable and a column variable.)

The subcommand **/STATISTICS CHISQ** tells SPSS/PC+ to produce the chi-square statistic, along with its associated degrees of freedom and significance level.

By default, each cell of the table will contain the number of cases for that particular cell. The subcommand **/CELLS** is used to specify additional cell contents. **COUNT** tells SPSS/PC+ to produce the number of cases for each cell. (This is produced by default even if you do not use the subcommand **/CELLS**.) **EXPECTED** tells SPSS/PC+ to produce the expected frequencies for each cell (the number of cases expected in each cell if the row variable and the column variable were independent). Other options that can be added include **ROW**, which calculates and prints percentages relative to the number of cases per row; **COLUMN**, which does likewise relative to columns; and **TOTAL**, which reports each cell in terms of the percentage of the total number of cases in the table. To obtain all of this information, specify the subcommand

```
/CELLS COUNT EXPECTED ROW COLUMN TOTAL
```

VISITORS by TREAT

| VISITORS | TREAT<br>Count<br>Exp Val | 1 | 2 | 3 | Page 1 of 1<br>Row<br>Total |
|---|---|---|---|---|---|
| | 1 | 9<br>3.7 | 3<br>4.7 | 1<br>4.7 | 13<br>33.3% |
| | 2 | 1<br>3.7 | 10<br>4.7 | 2<br>4.7 | 13<br>33.3% |
| | 3 | 1<br>3.7 | 1<br>4.7 | 11<br>4.7 | 13<br>33.3% |
| | Column<br>Total | 11<br>28.2% | 14<br>35.9% | 14<br>35.9% | 39<br>100.0% |

```
Chi-Square                      Value           DF        Significance
--------------------         -----------       ----       ------------

Pearson                      34.20779           4             .00000
Likelihood Ratio             32.87056           4             .00000
Mantel-Haenszel test for     19.11801           1             .00001
      linear association

Minimum Expected Frequency -    3.667
Cells with Expected Frequency < 5 -     9 OF     9 (100.0%)

Number of Missing Observations:  0
```

When you execute the **CROSSTABS** command, SPSS/PC+ produces a VISITORS by TREAT table. The table includes the count of cases and expected frequency for each cell. In addition, SPSS/PC+ produces column and row totals and percentages.

Next, chi-square test statistics are given, along with their associated degrees of freedom and significance levels. The chi-square statistic provides a test of the null hypothesis that the proportion of patients who receive excellent, fair, and poor treatment in nursing homes is the same for patients who receive frequent, occasional, and no visitors—in other words, that treatment quality is not related to visitation frequency.

The Pearson statistic is the most common test of the relationship between the two qualitative variables VISITORS and TREAT. The observed Pearson chi-square value is 34.21, and there are four degrees of freedom (the product of the number of columns minus one and the number of rows minus one). The associated *p*-value, labeled "Significance," is reported as .00000, which means it is less than .000005 and was rounded off. There is a significant relationship between the two variables. The other statistics reported are probably of no interest to you at this point.

• • • • • •

# Appendix A: Reading and Writing Command Files and Data Files

Throughout this manual we have explained the simplest way to enter your commands and data into SPSS/PC+; everything is simply typed into the Edit window within SPSS/PC+. This method is perfectly fine and is certainly the easiest to use if your data set is small and you do not wish to run many different analyses on different days. However, with "real" research data, one often has a large amount of data that will be analyzed in different ways at different times. Then it is very time-consuming and inefficient to retype all of your commands and all of your data every time you want to run some analyses. This appendix explains how command and data files can be stored as separate files on your computer or floppy disk for repeated use.

## Reading and Writing Command Files

If you have entered a large number of commands, along with your raw data, into the SPSS/PC+ Edit window, you might want to save the results of all this typing for another day. Once you leave SPSS/PC+, all the stuff that was in the Edit window is gone, so if you want to go back the next day and repeat your analysis or do some new analyses of the same data, you have to retype everything you had entered the day before. It would therefore be very useful if you could save what you typed into the Edit window and somehow read it back into SPSS/PC+ during a subsequent session. Fortunately, there is an easy way to do this.

At any point in your SPSS/PC+ session, you can save the current contents of the Edit window (i.e., your commands) by pressing F9. You will then see the words "Write Whole File" highlighted at the bottom of the screen. Press ENTER to select this, and type in a file name for the commands you wish to save (e.g., **A:ANOVA.SPS**, to save a file named "ANOVA.SPS" on your floppy disk in drive A). Everything in the Edit window at the time, including lines not currently visible on the screen, will be saved in the file you named. At some time later, after leaving SPSS/PC+, you can check to see that this file exists on your disk, and you can look at it using WordPerfect or any other text viewing or editing program.

Now, suppose you come back the next day and wish to run the same commands that you previously saved in ANOVA.SPS. After getting into SPSS/PC+ and hitting ALT-E (to switch into Edit mode), just hit F3. Then use the right arrow key to highlight the words "Insert File." Press ENTER to select this, and then type in the name of the file you wish to insert (in this case, **A:ANOVA.SPS**). The commands saved in that file now appear on the Edit screen as if you had just typed them in. You can proceed to edit them, execute them, or do anything else you would do if you had just typed them in.

If you so desire, you can also create or edit a command file using your favorite text editor or word processor, and then get into SPSS/PC+ and call the file into the Edit window using F3. (There is probably no advantage to doing things this way, however, unless your command file is very long and complicated.) Or, you can edit a command file previously written in SPSS/PC+ (and saved with F9) using your word processor, save the edited version, and later call it into SPSS/PC+ with F3.

There is one very important complication in using most word processors to edit command files, however. When you save a document in a word processor such as WordPerfect, the document is saved by default in a format or "language" that only that word processor understands. If you try to read this file into SPSS/PC+, it simply won't work. Instead, from your word processor you need to save the file in a special format, usually called an "ASCII" or "DOS" file, that SPSS/PC+, and many other programs, can understand. Most widely available word-processing programs offer a way to do this; consult the appropriate manual to find out how. For example, in DOS versions of WordPerfect, you would use the "Text In/Out" function key (Control-F5) rather than the "Exit" function key (F7). If you use DOS EDIT, you won't have this problem; the files it creates are automatically stored in ASCII format.

## *Reading and Writing Data Files*

In the examples in this manual, the raw data for each problem have been typed directly into SPSS/PC+ (between the **BEGIN DATA** and **END DATA** commands). With large data sets, however, it is often easier to create a separate file for your data by using WordPerfect (or another word processor), and then have SPSS/PC+ read the data from that file, rather than type it all into SPSS/PC+. Here's how:

*Step 1: Create the Data File.* Creating a data file using a word-processing program such as WordPerfect involves the same procedure as the one described earlier for creating a command file. Create the data file as you would any other document in your word processor, and save it as a DOS (ASCII) file. Be sure to remember the name of the file in which the data were saved; we recommend calling it "something.DAT"—for example, THESIS.DAT—where the .DAT extension will remind you that the file contains data. Also, note the information you will later need to write your **DATA LIST** command—namely, the format in which the data were entered (i.e., which variables are in which columns).

*Step 2: Read the Data with SPSS/PC+.* When you are ready to run some analyses on these data, get into SPSS/PC+ and switch into the Edit mode with ALT-E. Your first command, as usual, must be **DATA LIST**, so type the command in the usual way to specify the names of your variables and their column locations.

You need to make one modification to this command in order to tell SPSS/PC+ where to find the actual data. This is accomplished by inserting a **FILE = 'filename'** subcommand after the words **DATA LIST** and before the word **FIXED**. This command will specify the name of the file that contains the raw data; for example,

```
DATA LIST FILE='A:THESIS.DAT' FIXED / VAR1 1-2 VAR2 4-6.
```

tells SPSS/PC+ that the data are in a file called THESIS.DAT on the disk in drive A. (If your data file is being read from a disk, remember to specify, before the file name, which disk drive you are using.) The remainder of the command follows the usual rules for specifying the format of the data in that file.

Because you won't be typing the data directly into SPSS/PC+, there is no need to include a **BEGIN DATA** or **END DATA** command. Instead, you can proceed directly to the analyses you wish to conduct. For example, if the data for the one-sample *t*-test (see pages 20–25) were stored in a data file called SCORES.DAT on a diskette in drive A, the commands for the analysis would appear as follows:

```
DATA LIST FILE='SCORES.DAT' FIXED / STUDENT 1-2 IQ 4-6.
COMPUTE CONSTANT = 105.
T-TEST /PAIRS = IQ CONSTANT.
```

# Appendix B: SPSS/PC+ System Files

If you expect to analyze the same data repeatedly and don't wish to retype your **DATA LIST** and raw data every time, you may use a special kind of file called an SPSS/PC+ System File. It is a file that can be read or created only using SPSS/PC+. It is a fundamentally different kind of file from the command files and raw data files discussed previously.

## The SPSS/PC+ *SAVE* Command

At any given point during your SPSS/PC+ session, SPSS/PC+ has in its memory a thing called an "active file." This contains the raw data it read, the names of your variables, and the results of any data transformations done up to that point. For example, if you have created a new variable using the **COMPUTE** command, as was done in the previous one-sample *t*-test example, this variable is part of the active file along with your original variables. This information is being held in the computer's memory (RAM), so that when you request a statistical analysis, SPSS/PC+ merely consults this active file for all the information it needs. Each time you create a new variable or modify an existing one (see Appendix C), the active file is updated, so that at any given moment the active file contains the most up-to-date version of your data and related information. Once you leave SPSS/PC+, however, this file disappears forever. (If you get right back into SPSS/PC+ and issue **T-TEST** as your first command, for example, SPSS/PC+ will issue an error message telling you that it doesn't have any data to analyze. It doesn't remember anything about your previous session.)

At any point in your SPSS/PC+ session, you can issue a command to SPSS/PC+ to save the current active file in a more permanent format—namely, as a file on a hard disk or floppy disk. The command is simple:

```
SAVE /OUTFILE = 'filename'.
```

The name of the file you want to save is, of course, substituted for "filename." To save it as a file called THESIS.SYS on your diskette in drive A, for example, you would type

```
SAVE /OUTFILE = 'A:THESIS.SYS'.
```

and execute this command (with F10) as you would any other SPSS/PC+ command. (*Note:* It is a good idea to name your system files with a special suffix, such as .SYS, so you don't get these files confused with data files or command files on your diskette.) This new file will now contain all of the information about your data that was being held in the computer's memory at the time you issued the command.

## *The SPSS/PC+* ***GET*** *Command*

Now suppose on some later occasion you wish to run some more analyses on the same data. You need only to get into SPSS/PC+, switch to Edit mode (ALT-E), and type and execute (as usual, using F10) the following command:

```
GET /FILE = 'A:THESIS.SYS'.
```

SPSS/PC+ will now retrieve the system file THESIS.SYS from the disk in drive A and load it into its memory, exactly as it was at the moment you issued the **SAVE** command previously. You can simply pick up where you left off last time and run any analyses you wish; there is no need to write a **DATA LIST** command or enter any data. When you are finished, there is no need to resave the system file using **SAVE /OUTFILE**, unless you have made modifications to the active file and wish to replace the old version of THESIS.SYS with an updated version. If you just quit SPSS/PC+ without issuing a new **SAVE /OUTFILE** command, the system file THESIS.SYS will still be on your diskette as originally saved.

• • • • • •

# *Appendix C: Data Transformations*

With just one small exception (in the section on the one-sample *t*-test), all of the examples in this manual have assumed that the data for all of the variables are entered into SPSS/PC+ in ready-to-use form. In many situations, however, you might wish to create new variables from existing variables, or change the values of existing variables after the raw data have already been read into the program. SPSS/PC+ offers a variety of options for doing this. In this appendix, we briefly note a few of the most commonly used data transformation commands available in SPSS/PC+.

## *The* ***COMPUTE*** *Command*

In the section on one-sample *t*-tests, we introduced (but did not really explain) the **COMPUTE** command. In that case, we wanted to create a new variable for use in a subsequent procedure (**T-TEST**). Specifically, we wanted to create a variable called "CONSTANT" so that all of the subjects in our data set had a score of 105 on that variable. After the **DATA LIST**, **BEGIN DATA**, and **END DATA** commands, we inserted the command

```
COMPUTE CONSTANT = 105.
```

in order to accomplish this.

Note that, alternatively, we could have created these data "manually," without using the **COMPUTE** command, by simply treating CONSTANT as another variable in the raw data from the very beginning. For example, we could have added the number "105" to columns 8–10 of each line of data and added **CONSTANT 8-10** to the end of the **DATA LIST** command; then the variable CONSTANT would have been read by **DATA LIST** just like any other variable. However, using the **COMPUTE** command is much simpler in this case, saves a lot of typing, and decreases the likelihood of data-entry errors.

More typically, we wish to create new variables as functions of our other existing variables. For example, your raw data might consist of responses to five survey questions concerning some particular issue, and you wish to add up the responses to the five questions to construct a total attitude score. You could do this "manually" by adding up each subject's scores yourself and then entering the (hand-calculated) total scores into SPSS/PC+ from the beginning. Or you could enter the five original survey variables into SPSS/PC+ and then have SPSS/PC+ do the calculations for you. Your command file might look like this:

```
DATA LIST FIXED / Q1 1 Q2 3 Q3 5 Q4 7 Q5 9.
BEGIN DATA.

[lines of data here]

END DATA.
COMPUTE TOTAL = Q1 + Q2 + Q3 + Q4 + Q5.
```

After these commands are executed, each subject will have a score on the variable TOTAL, just as if you had calculated these TOTAL scores yourself and entered them directly into SPSS/PC+. Using the **COMPUTE** command offers two advantages, however, particularly if your data set is at all large: (1) It saves you the trouble of having to do all that arithmetic (which, after all, is something that computers are very good at), and (2) the computer will not make any errors in its calculations, and you probably will (at least, if you're like us).

You can specify virtually any kind of algebraic equation in a **COMPUTE** command to create a new variable as a function of existing ones. You always specify the name of the new variable first, followed by an equal sign, followed by an equation. Arithmetic operations are specified using + for addition, - for subtraction, * for multiplication, and / for division. SPSS/PC+ understands the standard rules for sequence of operations (e.g., multiplication and division before addition and subtraction), and parentheses can be used where needed (or just to make things clear). Note that you may insert extra spaces anywhere in the command, as we have done in the examples, to enhance readability, but this is not necessary.

As one additional example, suppose you want to create the total attitude score in the example given as the average (mean) of the first survey responses rather than the simple sum. Change the **COMPUTE** command given earlier to the following:

```
COMPUTE TOTAL = (Q1 + Q2 + Q3 + Q4 + Q5) / 5.
```

This command creates the new variable TOTAL by (for each subject) adding up the five survey responses and dividing this sum by 5.

For more information about use of the **COMPUTE** command, including more complex mathematical functions, see the appropriate SPSS/PC+ user's guide.

## The **RECODE** Command

The **RECODE** command is another handy data transformation command that allows you to change subjects' values on an existing variable. For example, suppose you had entered the data for the variable SEX with 1's representing men and 0's women, and then later for some reason you decided that you wanted to use 1's and 2's instead. Once the data have been read by SPSS/PC+, you could type and execute the following command:

```
RECODE SEX (0=1)(1=2).
```

This tells SPSS/PC+ to change, on the variable SEX, all of the 0's to 1's and all of the 1's to 2's. After this command is executed, your data are (inside SPSS/PC+) just as if you had entered 1's and 2's in the first place.

A **RECODE** command consists of the word **RECODE** followed immediately by the name(s) of one or more variables whose values you wish to change. Each set of parentheses specifies a "from" value and a "to" value separated by an equal sign. You may include as many sets of parentheses as you wish. You may specify up to three "from" values to be recoded to the same new "to" value. For example, suppose you had entered data on subjects' religious affiliation (RELIG) as 1 = Protestant, 2 = Catholic, 3 = other, and 4 = none. For the purpose of certain analyses, you might want to recode the variable into a dichotomy so that the "nones" are represented by 0's and everyone else by 1's. The following command would accomplish this:

```
RECODE RELIG (2,3=1)(4=0).
```

Notice that there is no need to specify (1=1); any values not specified for recoding remain unchanged. However, you may include (1=1) if doing so makes you feel better. (We often do this ourselves, just for a sense of closure.)

## The **IF** Command

In some cases you may wish to transform existing variables or create new variables, but you wish to do so only for some subjects or differently for different subjects. The **IF** command makes this possible. An **IF** command looks like this:

```
IF (VARA = 1) VARB = 7.
```

The part in parentheses specifies the conditions under which the computation is to be performed; in this case, VARB will be assigned a value of 7 only for those subjects who have a score of 1 on VARA.

Alternatively, you may use any of the following in place of the equal sign within parentheses: < (less than), > (greater than), <= (less than or equal to), or >= (greater than or equal to). For example, the command

```
IF (VARA >= 1) VARB = 7.
```

assigns the variable VARB a value of 7 if VARA is greater than or equal to 1.

The part after the parentheses specifies the computation to be performed if the condition is met; this part is very much like (and follows the same rules as) the **COMPUTE** command. The variable being modified (VARB in this case) may be either a new variable or an existing variable.

## *The **SELECT IF** and **PROCESS IF** Commands*

The **SELECT IF** command is used to restrict one or more analyses to a specified subset of subjects. For example,

```
SELECT IF (SEX = 1).
```

tells SPSS/PC+ to select from the data set only those subjects that have a value of 1 on the variable SEX. The rules for specifying conditions within parentheses are the same as for the **IF** command above. Thus, you may use <, >, <=, or >= in place of = if appropriate.

Once a **SELECT IF** command is executed, it remains in effect for the remainder of that SPSS/PC+ session. That is, once the command above is executed, all subsequent commands and procedures will be restricted to subjects with SEX equal to 1. To restore the data set to its original (complete) state, you need to rerun your **DATA LIST** (or **GET FILE**) command and reread the data.

If you wish to temporarily select a subset of cases for just a single analysis or procedure, use the command **PROCESS IF** instead. The format is the same as for **SELECT IF**—for example,

```
PROCESS IF (SEX = 1).
```

This command tells SPSS/PC+ to include, for the *next* statistical procedure (e.g., **T-TEST**, **CORRELATIONS**) executed only, just those subjects for whom the variable SEX = 1. After the next procedure is completed, the data set is restored to its original condition.

For example, if you want to run a particular procedure separately for males and for females, you could use **PROCESS IF** as illustrated here:

```
PROCESS IF (SEX = 1).
CORRELATIONS X Y.
PROCESS IF (SEX = 2).
CORRELATIONS X Y.
```

Notice that this command sequence would not work properly if you had used **SELECT IF** rather than **PROCESS IF** for the first command. Because the changes executed by **SELECT IF** remain in effect for the remainder of the session, there would be no subjects in the data set for whom SEX = 2 by the time SPSS/PC+ got to the third command in the sequence.

TO THE OWNER OF THIS BOOK:

We hope that you have found *A Simple Guide to SSPS/PC+ for Versions 4.0 and 5.0* useful. So that this book can be improved in a future edition, would you take the time to complete this sheet and return it? We'd really like to hear what you think.

School and address: ____________________

Department: ____________________

Instructor's name: ____________________

1. What I like most about this book is: ____________________

____________________

____________________

2. What I like least about this book is: ____________________

____________________

____________________

3. My general reaction to this book is: ____________________

____________________

4. The name of the course in which I used this book is: ____________________

____________________

____________________

5. In the space below, or on a separate sheet of paper, please write specific suggestions for improving this book and anything else you'd care to share about your experience in using the book.

____________________

____________________

____________________

____________________

____________________

____________________

Optional:

Your name: ______________________________ Date: ______________________________

May Brooks/Cole quote you, either in promotion for *A Simple Guide to SSPS/PC+* or in future publishing ventures?

Yes: __________ No: __________

Sincerely,

*Lee A. Kirkpatrick*
*Brooke C. Feeney*

FOLD HERE

NO POSTAG
NECESSAR
IF MAILED
IN THE
UNITED STAT

**BUSINESS REPLY MAIL**
FIRST CLASS PERMIT NO. 358 PACIFIC GROVE, CA

POSTAGE WILL BE PAID BY ADDRESSEE

ATT: *Lee A. Kirkpatrick and Brooke C. Feeney*

**Brooks/Cole Publishing Company**
**511 Forest Lodge Road**
**Pacific Grove, California 93950-9968**

FOLD HERE